Tennessee

A Bicentennial History

Wilma Dykeman

W. W. Norton & Company, Inc.
New York

American Association for State and Local History
Nashville

Copyright © 1975
American Association for State and Local History
Nashville, Tennessee

Library of Congress Cataloguing-in-Publication Data

Dykeman, Wilma.
  Tennessee, a bicentennial history.

  (States and the Nation)
  Bibliography: p.
  1. Tennessee—History. I. Title. II. Series.
F436.D983 1975   976.8   75–25873
ISBN 0–393–05555–8
          Printed in the United States of America

This book is for

a special Tennessean:

James

Contents

Illustrations

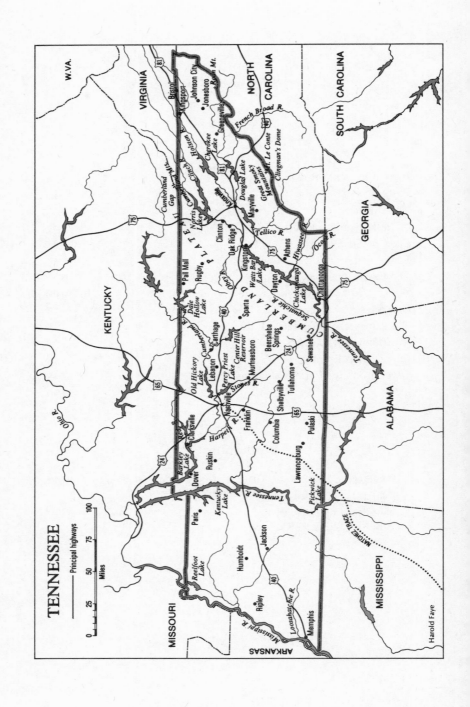

TENNESSEE

—— Principal highways

Miles

0   25   50   75   100

Harold Faye

Invitation to the Reader

IN 1807, former President John Adams argued that a complete history of the American Revolution could not be written until the history of change in each state was known, because the principles of the Revolution were as various as the states that went through it. Two hundred years after the Declaration of Independence, the American nation has spread over a continent and beyond. The states have grown in number from thirteen to fifty. And democratic principles have been interpreted differently in every one of them.

We therefore invite you to consider that the history of your state may have more to do with the bicentennial review of the American Revolution than does the story of Bunker Hill or Valley Forge. The Revolution has continued as Americans extended liberty and democracy over a vast territory. John Adams was right: the states are part of that story, and the story is incomplete without an account of their diversity.

The Declaration of Independence stressed life, liberty, and the pursuit of happiness; accordingly, it shattered the notion of holding new territories in the subordinate status of colonies. The Northwest Ordinance of 1787 set forth a procedure for new states to enter the Union on an equal footing with the old. The Federal Constitution shortly confirmed this novel means of building a nation out of equal states. The step-by-step process through which territories have achieved self-government and national representation is among the most important of the Founding Fathers' legacies.

The method of state-making reconciled the ancient conflict between liberty and empire, resulting in what Thomas Jefferson called an empire for liberty. The system has worked and remains unaltered, despite enormous changes that have taken

place in the nation. The country's extent and variety now sur-
pass anything the patriots of '76 could likely have imagined.
The United States has changed from an agrarian republic into a
highly industrial and urban democracy, from a fledgling nation
into a major world power. As Oliver Wendell Holmes remarked
in 1920, the creators of the nation could not have seen completely how it and its constitution and its states would develop.
Any meaningful review in the bicentennial era must consider
what the country has become, as well as what it was.

The new nation of equal states took as its motto *E Pluribus
Unum*—"out of many, one." But just as many peoples have
become Americans without complete loss of ethnic and cultural
identities, so have the states retained differences of character.
Some have been superficial, expressed in stereotyped images—
big, boastful Texas, "sophisticated" New York, "hillbilly"
Arkansas. Other differences have been more real, sometimes instructively, sometimes amusingly; democracy has embraced
Huey Long's Louisiana, bilingual New Mexico, unicameral Nebraska, and a Texas that once taxed fortunetellers and spawned
politicians called "Woodpecker Republicans" and "Skunk
Democrats." Some differences have been profound, as when
South Carolina secessionists led other states out of the Union in
opposition to abolitionists in Massachusetts and Ohio. The result was a bitter Civil War.

The Revolution's first shots may have sounded in Lexington
and Concord; but fights over what democracy should mean and
who should have independence have erupted from Pennsylvania's Gettysburg to the "Bleeding Kansas" of John Brown,
from the Alamo in Texas to the Indian battles at Montana's
Little Bighorn. Utah Mormons have known the strain of isolation; Hawaiians at Pearl Harbor, the terror of attack; Georgians
during Sherman's march, the sadness of defeat and devastation.
Each state's experience differs instructively; each adds understanding to the whole.

The purpose of this series of books is to make that kind of understanding accessible, in a way that will last in value far
beyond the bicentennial fireworks. The series offers a volume
on every state, plus the District of Columbia—fifty-one, in all.

Each book contains, besides the text, a view of the state through eyes other than the author's—a "photographer's essay," in which a skilled photographer presents his own personal perceptions of the state's contemporary flavor.

We have asked authors not for comprehensive chronicles, nor for research monographs or new data for scholars. Bibliographies and footnotes are minimal. We have asked each author for a summing up—interpretive, sensitive, thoughtful, individual, even personal—of what seems significant about his or her state's history. What distinguishes it? What has mattered about it, to its own people and to the rest of the nation? What has it come to now?

To interpret the states in all their variety, we have sought a variety of backgrounds in authors themselves and have encouraged variety in the approaches they take. They have in common only these things: historical knowledge, writing skill, and strong personal feelings about a particular state. Each has wide latitude for the use of the short space. And if each succeeds, it will be by offering you, in your capacity as a *citizen* of a state *and* of a nation, stimulating insights to test against your own.

James Morton Smith
General Editor

Preface

$\mathcal{T}$HIS is a history of Tennessee in only the most limited, perhaps the most generous, use of the term. A more accurate description might be a portrait of Tennessee.

Definitive history must be inclusive. The page limitations determined that this book should be exclusive. The challenge and frustration of the task became one of choices. Through such choices, *Tennessee* became a personal interpretation more than an academic compilation.

Methods of scholarly research and the most painstaking accuracy in facts and figures were not sacrificed in this process. Perhaps they were given special attention because the other feature balancing this portrait was its need to be readable, to include anecdote that could clarify statistic, character study that would enrich insight. Tennesseans have been too worthy to have their history distorted; they have been too lively to have their history consigned to the past.

Therefore it has seemed to me less important to list every well-known historic event or to name every familiar famous person than to bring to life some of those who lived well, worked hard, struggled courageously—or, on the other hand, some who brought style, dash, flavor, a special bravura to their time and place.

There was also the fact to remember that this portrait is part of our national Bicentennial observation, one of fifty that will compose a full-length portrait of the United States of America. Because of this, my goal has been to discover as accurately as possible what was distinctly Tennessean and also what was characteristically American in the state's past and present.

This account is more or less chronological through chapter 5, on the Civil War. Then the progression becomes topical, although a loose time sequence may be discerned. This shift is not the result of caprice, but of necessity, the need to encompass as completely as possible the cumulative events and effects of the state's accelerating history. While the rather stately succession of generations provides a satisfactory unifying force until the giant cataclysm of Civil War, from that point on, the increasing tempo and variety of the Tennessee experience seems to demand unification through subjects—such as politics, religion, music, education, culture, urbanization, etc. Thus influences from the past gather into realities of the present.

Contemplating the future, I have come to the conclusion that we may approach a new understanding and release when we free ourselves of the myth of retrogression.

We were not born of saints; we do not descend from a race of the spotless anointed. Somewhere between yesterday and today, there was not a special interval during which a dramatis personae of heroines and heroes was whisked from a stage called "Tennessee" and a cast of lesser characters substituted. The men and women who have measured up to new needs and changing conditions within these boundaries were just that— men and women: stout and frail, honorable and venal, courageous and fearful, rendered wise by optimistic faith and pragmatic experience and knowledge of their heritage, or callous by cynicism, apathy, and greed.

The drama and impact of their adventure and our inheritance lies in its intense humanity—in conflict with outside forces, in conflict with itself. The miracle is not whether a chosen group of super-people called "pioneers" or "ancestors"—with a few villains salted in for contrast and spice—once lived, labored, and died here. The wonder is that so-called average men and women of many races and nations reddened plots of earth with their blood, soaked tons of garments, tools, and weapons with their sweat, spent tears of agony and triumph, enduring and meeting a great challenge as they saw it.

They did not always see that challenge plain—or whole. Perceived pressures of immediate survival often bred astigmatism of long-range philosophic vision. Niceties of personal conscience or considerations of the future became blurred by necessities of immediate community welfare. The message of many of their choices, wise and unwise, is still writ large for us to read today.

It is time, then, to free ourselves of fictitious guilt, the guilt of our own inferiority when measured against giants of our recreated past, the guilt of retrogression. They blazed a trail, sometimes grandly, sometimes shoddily, frequently at costly expense of life. And the trail has become history's highway, our own. Without exaggeration or sentimentality, we can survey the totality of the course, its peaks and plunges and meanderings, to discover past and present frontiers and recognize their meaning for those appearing on the next century's horizons.

Wilma Dykeman Stokely

March 1975

Tennessee

1

The Place

ALL Tennessee, like Caesar's Gaul, is divided into three parts.

Tennesseans visiting other regions and countries seldom identify their home state by its name alone. Their usual response: "I live in West Tennessee," or "My home is in Middle Tennessee," or "I'm from East Tennessee."

This is no idle conversational gambit, no exercise in petty provincialism. It is a statement of geography which is also a condensation of history, a reminder of sociology, a hint of cultural variety shaped by geographical fact: for, if there is unity in Tennessee's diversity, there is also tension and suspicion, humor and individuality, and above all, tenacity and vitality. From the first probing European thrust inland to the land of the western waters and its settlement, to the latest project for "development" of that land, day after tomorrow, the passage of time and events has not so much extinguished or renounced those three natural divisions as it has enunciated and magnified them.

What, then, is this unit, this triumvirate, known as Tennessee? It is a rough parallelogram, 432 miles long and approximately 110 miles wide, bracketed between some of the tallest mountains in eastern America and the largest river on the continent, exemplifying the dual features of the truism that mountains lock in, rivers lead out.

First and last, it is land—land rich with the loam of centuries, land spread thin over knobby hills, land supporting majestic virgin forests and succulent grasses and abundant crops. The land is piled up in eastern mountain ranges offering such variety of scenery, habitat and climate that the abundant life of trees, plants, animals, birds, and fish is surpassed only by the human diversity that has sought out this territory in annually increasing multitudes. Seven million came in 1974, giving the Great Smoky Mountains National Park more visitors than any other national park in the United States. The land rolls across Middle Tennessee, hills and meadows and bluegrass country. The land levels toward the west, brooding, alternately secret and open in the depths of tangled woods, the broad expanse of rich, yielding fertility of centuries.

Was it free land as much as—perhaps more than—freedom of religion that brought and held those first tenacious settlers? Wise old Bishop Francis Asbury, who traveled the western back country through more than a dozen years at the end of the eighteenth century, knew the power of land on the people among whom he labored. On a Saturday late in March 1797, after scaling "rocks, hills and mountains, worming through pathless woods," and finally riding down a steep slope "hit or miss, Providence is all," the weary Bishop wrote in his Journal: "I am of opinion it is hard, or harder, for the people of the west to gain religion as any other. . . . when I reflect that not one in a hundred came here to get religion, but rather to get plenty of good land, I think it will be well if some or many do not eventually lose their souls." [1]

Tennesseans gave names to their land, its rivers and hills, valleys and coves, crossroads and cities. They were grandiose names, playful, original, borrowed; names rich with connotation of heritage from many peoples, musical in their rhythm, amusing in their bluntness. Through the names left on this land, the Indian presence endures: from that of the state itself and the limpid flow of *Loosahatchie, Chattanooga, Ooltewah,* to the dis-

---

1. Samuel Cole Williams, *Early Travels in the Tennessee Country, 1540–1800* (Johnson City, Tenn.: Watauga, 1928), p. 305.

tinction of *Tuckaleechee* and *Chilhowee, Unaka, Chickamauga.*
There is English solidity in *Cumberland,* tribute to ancient glory
in *Memphis, Sparta, Athens.* Heroes and heroines, national and
local, remembered and forgotten, flourish in hundreds of names
scattered like mustard seeds that took root and flowered—
from *Dandridge* town, (named for Martha, George Washington's wife), to *Crockett* County, (named for Davy himself);
from *Bean's Station,* (for William Bean, in 1769 the earliest
settler in the Tennessee country), to *Humboldt,* (honoring a German naturalist). There are reminders of humor and hardship in
names of *Curve* and *Defeated, Huggins Hell* and *Fodderstack
Mountain* and *Rattling Cave.* In names laden with meaning, the
land stretches sad and proud not only in distance but in time:
Sycamore Shoals to *Land Between the Lakes, Fort Prudhomme*
to *Tullahoma, Shiloh* to *Clinton,* and hundreds of other names
find distinctive echo in each individual memory.

The land appeared immense and impersonal, but it became
slowly, surely, intensely personal to those who belonged to
it—and wished to make it belong to them. There was, for example, the new charter granted the town of Ripley, seat of
Lauderdale County, in 1901. When the corporate limits were
outlined, they included this notation: "Thence north 85 degrees,
east to a black gum marked with a cross and with mistletoe in
the top, and with a blue bird sitting on a limb, which is a short
distance east of Ed Johnson's horse lot." [2] This was land not
only incorporated, but embraced.

This Tennessee land is equalled only by Missouri in sharing
borders with more states than any other in the Union: North
Carolina to the east, Georgia, Alabama, and Mississippi on the
south, Kentucky and Virginia on the north, and Arkansas and
Missouri across the Mississippi River to the west. Each of these
neighbors exerts and receives an influence. In West Tennessee,
it has long been said that the Mississippi Delta begins in the
lobby of Memphis's Peabody Hotel and ends at Vicksburg.
Nashville is looked to as the metropolis of south-central Ken-

---

2. Federal Writers' Project, *Tennessee: A Guide to the State* (New York: Viking
Press, 1939), p. 422.

tucky. The suggestion has been made from time to time that the highlands of western North Carolina and eastern Tennessee should shake free of any lowland domination and form their own state of Transylvania. And Chattanooga's southern city limit coincides with the state's own boundary, a fact discovered by one general, encamped there during the Civil War, who found his headquarters to be in Tennessee while his troops bivouacked in Georgia. He learned that outlaws who rendezvoused in the vicinity evaded the law simply by stepping across the state line and out of an officer's reach.

"To reach across this imaginary line," General John Beatty wrote, "and draw a man back would be kidnapping, an insult to a sovereign state, and in a States' rights country such a procedure could not be tolerated. Requisitions from the governors of Tennessee and Georgia might, of course, be procured, but this would take time, and in this time, the offender could walk leisurely into Alabama or North Carolina, neither of which state is very far away." [3]

Within Tennessee's 42,244 square miles are more large and navigable waterways than in any other southern state, and—so the boast runs—every shape of beast and bug, every variety of tree and flower found from the blue waters of the Gulf to the somber, snow-laden forests of Canada. Indeed, it is a place of contrasts. Even its geography is both old and new: from the rose and purple rhododendron covering the slopes of ancient wind-swept Roan Mountain, 6,313 feet tall on the northeastern border, to the murky waters of Reelfoot Lake in the northwest, born in a giant upheaval of the New Madrid earthquake between December 16, 1811, and March 15, 1812, when the ground sank, trees were whirled away, and the Mississippi reversed its current to fill the depression in a series of mountainous waves. And as the fishermen and hunters around Reelfoot today have found a way of life based on the waters and swamps of this tangled, forested world of cypress and wild grapevines and water lilies and all manner of fish and fowl, so some of the

3. Gilbert E. Govan and James W. Livingood, *Chattanooga Country: From Toma-hawks to TVA* (New York: Dutton, 1952), p. 411.

mountain people living in the shadow of the Roan have searched out rare herbs such as ginseng and more common medicinals—Solomon's seal, black cohosh, and others—for markets as distant as China.

East Tennessee includes three subregions: the Unakas and Great Smokies, a rugged spine of lofty, tree-covered pinnacles, many reaching more than 6,000 feet along the horizon; the Great Valley, a continuation of Virginia's pleasant Shenandoah, harboring much of the state's fertile farmland and two of its largest cities, Knoxville and Chattanooga; and the Cumberland Plateau, an Appalachian rampart indented with deep valleys, including one bold irregularity, a broad cove known as the Sequatchie Valley, which slants almost halfway across the state.

Middle Tennessee is made up of the Highland Rim, sometimes called the Barrens, characterized by many streams and ravines and embracing another region, the Central Basin. With Nashville as its self-styled "dimple," the Basin is one of the finest agricultural areas in the state, resembling the vast bed of a drained lake. Underlying limestone nourishes grasses that combine with climate and water to produce excellent livestock, especially horses—including the famous Tennessee walking horse.

West Tennessee contains the Coastal Plain, composed of the Plateau and the Mississippi Bottoms, offering that luxuriant growth of timber and cotton that became outstanding features of the economy and culture distinguishing Tennessee's largest city. Memphis has been renowned in fact and fiction for its riverfront cotton exchange, and it remains today the hardwood manufacturing center of the world.

To identify the regions of Tennessee, however, is merely to place us in geography; it does not evoke the presence of their rich and distinctive life. Ultimately, that presence cannot be experienced through words, but only by that learning which poet Allen Tate has described as "knowledge carried to the heart."

Such knowledge is won through the senses: sight of blue, hickory-wood smoke rising from a mud-daubed chimney up an isolated Appalachian cove, or a winter sun disappearing westward, trailing scarlet sashes across the sky above a Memphis

skyscraper; sounds of Saturday night in gaudy back-alley-
honky-tonks replaced by the timeless call of Sunday morning
church chimes flowing like honey over drowsy courthouse
towns and clustered city blocks; smell of black river-bottom
earth submerged by flood, a redolence acrid and fetid with pri-
meval fertility, and odors of cedar fencerows and pine woods in
the stillness of high noon, of tobacco curing to golden brown in
autumn barns, of spring honeysuckle and newly cut summer
grass; taste of wild blackberries and winesap apples from the
hills and sun-ripened strawberries from the lowlands, of crisply
crusted catfish and hush-puppies, succulent ham and red-eye
gravy, the common pungency of collard greens, sweet potatoes,
white "soup" beans, cornbread baked in ironware from freshly
ground meal, plus the subtle savor of mountain trout in butter,
syllabub and Sally Lunn and great-grandmother's special am-
brosia; touch of fresh wind ushering rain-clouds after a long
drought over scalded strips of interstate highways and parched
hay fields, feel of emerald woods-moss velvety against the
hand, and knife-sharp blades of dried corn fodder, prick of late-
summer Spanish needles, snow slashing against the face atop
Mt. LeConte or Clingman's Dome in January, and heat burning
arms and neck in a July cotton field.

Such knowledge is distilled by memory. It may be contained
in the journal of a British visitor who tried to impart to his
fellow countrymen the incredible vastness and fertility of the
earth he beheld beside the Mississippi in 1761: "The land is so
rich and the soil so deep that in many places one may run a soldier's pike up to the head without meeting a rock or stone and
capable of producing everything." It is suggested in the breath-
less account of a captain of the French marines who beheld
along the Mississippi in 1752 "whole clouds of pigeons" so
thick that their passing "often eclipsed the sun." [4]

Or the knowledge may be rendered through the understanding
of a sensitive historian such as Harriette Simpson Arnow, who
wrote of the small hill-and-valley farms along the Cumberland
River:

4. Samuel Cole Williams, *Beginnings of West Tennessee* (Johnson City, Tenn.: Watauga, 1930), pp. 15, 28.

Crops and barns lie below them; above are pasture fields, below or around is the orchard with beehives . . . Each thing suited to its particular location. Such a farm has a quality unknown in any other for it feels the changing shape of hill shadow; the winter afternoons when all below lies cold and blue and the creek pools slowly skim with ice, the upper slopes are warm and bright; or on another farm the child coming home from school on the southern side of a hill steps from a snowless world of sunshine into a snowy waste of limestone crag and undripping icicles that lie above his northwardly sloping home.[5]

The knowledge may be shared in the memoir of a native son, Carl T. Rowan, born and reared in Middle Tennessee, reporting for the *Minneapolis Morning Tribune*. On a return to his hometown in 1951, he remembered the years of the depression "when eggs were a penny apiece there, but our pennies always were scarcer than hens' eggs." Grease and flour could make a skillet of gravy "that was at least filling, if neither appetizing nor nourishing." The white salt pork that was their basic fare they called "Hoover's ham." [6]

Knowledge of Tennessee was captured in novelist Evelyn Scott's memory of a day once central to community life across the state:

Seurat should have had a go at Clarksville on a court day . . . With the glare of high noon falling through the maples in a subtle rain of darkness (which was light, also, and brilliant) and squatting groups everywhere in the green; and, in the street, wagons and rickety vehicles, shafts on the ground; the animals, unharnessed, relieving disconsolate patience with surreptitious nibblings at forbidden vegetation. . . . There was a smell about court days—manure, sweat, watermelons, horses, mules and tobacco! The aroma of a circus—an odour of life! Court days, somehow, always seemed the hottest of the summer! [7]

Exaggeration and affection combine to fasten Donald Davidson's Tennessee River in the mind. To navigate the Tennessee,

5. Harriette Simpson Arnow, *Seedtime on the Cumberland* (New York: Macmillan, 1960), p. 39.

6. Carl T. Rowan, *South of Freedom* (New York: Knopf, 1954), p. 20.

7. Evelyn Scott, *Background in Tennessee* (New York: Robert M. McBride, 1937), p. 217.

he wrote that one needed not only the abilities of horse and alligator, but also the special talents of the frog, the snapping turtle, the raccoon, buffalo, and shikepoke.

Tennesseans, even at their most rebellious, have tended to bear a strong allegiance to their place. Perhaps this sense was embedded early and firmly by the fact that, for long generations, Tennesseans were an outdoor people. This was true not only for the hunters, trappers, surveyors, farmers, lumbermen, but for most of the professionals as well. Preachers "pastored" several churches, or followed arduous circuits in their struggle to tame the unfettered spirits of a civilization-in-the-shaping. Merchants made long trips by horseback and then by wagon to accumulate goods for trade and profit in burgeoning towns and crossroads. Doctors threw their saddlebags across a sturdy horse and rode in sleet or sun to tend the sick and afflicted, while lawyers traveled to many parts of the state in their bouts to heal society's ills and individuals' conflicts. People were familiar with woods and fields and pastures, went to mill and blacksmith, store and county seat and brush-arbor meeting and schoolhouse—and along the way, they all came to know the terrain, its soil and plants, the weather and its variations, and houses and landmarks. Their place became real, became their own.

There have been many jokes about this sense of place and Tennesseans: black and white, from mountains or lowlands, male or female, transplanted to other parts of the United States. One story familiar in Cleveland and Detroit and other northern cities, where the money-tree is reputed to grow, involves a man who died and went to heaven. All was beautiful and as he'd expected—except for one large group of people who were chained to trees. The newcomer asked who these people were, and St. Peter replied, "Those are Tennesseans. It's Friday, and we have to chain them to keep them from going back home for the weekend."

"Back home" has been of more than passing significance in many situations. During the Civil War, for example, the Confederate government published medical regulations listing various diseases that might afflict certain Southern troops. One of those named was "Nostalgia." And nostalgia removed many Tennesseans from the ranks in that conflict.

Later, it assured one East Tennessean of remaining in his home. When an elderly resident of the Great Smokies learned that a national park was to be established in his mountains, he petitioned the authorities for permission to be left in his home. He explained that he was partially blind and had learned to care for himself, get around his place, outdoors as well as in, by the feel of things—the shape of a rock, a rise in the ground; how could he learn another place at his age? He was allowed to stay.

Perhaps one of the most compelling experiences indicating this love of place concerned a Middle Tennessee boy who once complained, in the presence of his grandfather, of muddy drinking water and was sharply reprimanded: "Remember, you're drinking the sacred soil of your native land!"

This, then, is the place—stretching from the spacious green gateway of Cumberland Gap on its northeastern boundary to the sweeping passage of the mighty Mississippi along its western limits; from the harsh wilderness haunts of the fierce wild boar to the tangled, somnolent habitat of the lurking cottonmouth, from the high lonesome twang of "Barbara Allen" to the hurtling rhythm of "Casey Jones" and the syncopated sadness of "Beale Street Blues"—containing three geographies, three memories, three regions.

These three divisions are a basis for much of Tennessee's distinctive role in the history of America, a role bearing twin themes of frontier and border state.

From the days of DeSoto's daring push to the Mississippi across part of this landscape—more improbable and uncertain in many ways than Neil Armstrong's moon-walk—with his armored, quarrelsome, ruthless adventurers and their fever for gold, their horses, their droves of grunting, rooting, foraging swine, to the present moment of radiation research in the anonymous, impersonal laboratories of Oak Ridge, Tennessee has been a frontier. If that frontier's most picturesque symbol is Davy Crockett, who was not born on a mountaintop at all but on meandering Limestone Creek in Greene County, and who was accustomed to the formal black coat of the congressman as well as the buckskins of the trapper and hunter, perhaps the frontier's best-known twentieth-century symbol is found in that stairway of TVA dams that contains and controls the waters of the mighty Tennessee River and its network of tributaries, forming the Great Lakes of the South and a 10,000-mile shoreline, producing more power than is used by the entire nation of Italy.

In addition to the frontier nature of its experience, Tennessee has also been a border state. Its position as a border area between North and South has been recognized. Before Europeans ever arrived on the scene, trails worn into veritable highways laced the Tennessee country, made by the great Indian nations traveling up and down in their constant wars. Northern and southern factions were in conflict long before the first black man arrived in the hold of a slave ship. The Ohio River was a boundary marker for the northern and southern tribes, who travelled up and down it for centuries, hunting and making war.

Later Americans engaged in their own civil warfare would find Tennessee the crucial crossroads for Northern and Southern control of rail lines, food supplies, communications, and psychological solidarity. Still later, the popular Governor Bob Taylor dealt with Tennessee's North-South border reality in a lighter vein when he declaimed: "Mason and Dixon's line is still there, but it is only the dividing line between cold bread and hot biscuits, and there it will remain as long as the Yankee says, 'You hadn't ought to do it,' and the Southerner says, 'I've done done it!' " [8]

Less recognized, but of equal importance, there has been Tennessee's role as East-West border. Long before the differences between Yankee abolitionists and Dixie planters tore Tennesseans asunder and forced them to choose in blood between northern blue uniforms and southern grey within their own boundaries, tensions flourished between eastern seats of government power in Virginia and North Carolina, with their status quo of indifference to the back country, and the settlements on the western waters with their surge for independence. Tennessee was at the heart of the Old Southwest—and that fact has emphasized in the place and its people many qualities that we consider especially and characteristically American.

8. James P. Taylor, Alf A. Taylor, and Hugh L. Taylor, *Life and Career of Senator Robert Love Taylor* (Nashville: Bob Taylor Publishers, 1913), p. 197.

To understand Tennessee, it is necessary to understand this East-West conflict. For Tennessee was not one of the original thirteen states. The very names of its neighbors reflected English ancestry—indeed, English royalty. But Tennessee took its name from a river, and like that of so many of its other rivers— the Nolichucky and Ocoee, Tellico and Hiwassee and Sequatchie—that name recognized the Indian presence and heritage. As a stepchild of North Carolina, the Tennessee country endured—perhaps, at times, enjoyed—a long and stormy career in its search for identity.

The touchstone of that search was, once and always, independence. The fact that, during one short period of twenty-seven years, Tennesseans lived under nine forms of government may make them appear erratic and uncertain of what they wanted; nothing could be further from the truth. In reality, it is surprising to discover just how well these early citizens understood what they wanted government to be and do. It was their peculiar situation—as remote and hazardous back country to a distant, preoccupied state government in the east—that combined with a series of developing circumstances—land speculation, Indian treaties, the Revolutionary War—to lead them through the trial and error of roles as diverse as British colony, "Tributary to the Indians," Watauga Association, Washington District of North Carolina, Washington County, the State of Franklin, Washington County, again, the Territory of the United States South of the River Ohio, and, finally—on June 1, 1796—the State of Tennessee.

It was in East Tennessee, called the "seedbed of the west in politics," that the early settlers on the Watauga River gathered in the spring of 1772 and formed themselves into what history records as the first American attempt at complete self-government, the Watauga Association. Aware of their predicament as a frontier far removed from proper courts and legislature, they formed a court of five members, a sheriff, and a clerk, a move accomplished—and this was of paramount importance—"by the consent of every individual." Self-government—with as little government as possible—conducted by the democratic will of the majority: this was central to the Watauga Association and to every other effort the people of the Tennessee country made in their restlessness to be independent of the eastern North Carolina capital.

At least one official glimpsed the import of the Watauga Association and its petition. The Earl of Dunmore, last British governor of Virginia, wrote to the British Secretary of State that "a set of people" in the back country "have appointed magistrates and framed laws" and to all intents and purposes erected themselves into a separate state, thereby setting "a dangerous example to the people of America, of forming governments distinct from and independent of his majesty's authority." [9]

The perceptive Earl understood something else about these Americans: he spoke of their fondness for migration.

For the large numbers of them who were Scotch-Irish, migration was evidence, less of natural "fondness," perhaps, than of historic necessity. They had been on the move for a long time—since James I of England colonized nine counties in northern Ireland with Presbyterians from the Scottish Lowlands. These Scots—along with a few English, French, and Irish neighbors—worked hard and prospered. When they progressed enough to become competitive with English industry, however, their initiative was curbed by oppressive laws. Taxes, unusually harsh winters, potato crop failures, epidemics among the livestock, and economic repression pushed them to seek out a new land. They came by the dozens, the hundreds, the thousands, the great majority of them landing at Philadelphia. If their forbears had subscribed to the belief that "the best roads in Scotland were those leading out of it," they extended that opinion to the roads of northern Ireland.

From Pennsylvania, many found their way along Virginia's Shenandoah and into the Valley of East Tennessee. Others who went from Philadelphia on a more direct route south into the North Carolina Piedmont were the source of subsequent migrations from middle Carolina westward into the Tennessee country. There were many English, some Germans—mainly from

9. Mary French Caldwell, *Tennessee, the Dangerous Example: Watauga to 1849* (Nashville: Aurora Publishers, 1974), p. 29.

the Palatinate—and Welsh and Irish, a few Huguenots; but the dominant character of Tennesseans came to be identified with that of the Scotch-Irish. Fondness for migration was only one of their characteristics.

Tennessee historian John Trotwood Moore listed others: "If abused, they fight; if their rights are infringed they rebel; if forced, they strike; and if their liberties are threatened, they murder. They eat meat and always their bread is hot." [10]

Early in the history of this western country, a thoughtful Spaniard, Baron Carondelet, Governor of Louisiana, pondered the hardy breed that was pushing its conquest of the land to the great valley his own kingdom claimed. Writing to a friend in Spain in 1794 he spoke of "the immoderate ambition of a new people, adventurous and hostile to all subjection." They were a "vast and restless population" whose

> mode of growth and policy are as formidable to Spain as their arms. Their roving disposition and the readiness with which this people procure sustenance and shelter, facilitates rapid settlement. A rifle and a little corn meal in a bag is sufficient for an American wandering alone in the woods for a month. . . . with tree trunks placed transversely he forms a house, and even as impregnable fort against the Indians, building a second story above the first. The cold does not terrify him, and when a family grows weary of one locality, it moves to another and settles there with the same ease. [11]

The Spanish sought to take advantage of the independent spirit of early dwellers in the Tennessee country. If the dissatisfaction of these inhabitants could be effectively nurtured into separation from British influence, and then subsequently the colonial government, to their east, perhaps they could be won to support of Spanish claims for the Mississippi country. But such a flirtation failed—in large part, because these people did not want to exchange one far-removed and indifferent government for another; they wanted to be rid of all such rule.

What they were, they have in part remained: secessionists par

---

10. John Trotwood Moore and Austin P. Foster, *Tennessee, the Volunteer State* (Nashville and Chicago: S. J. Clarke, 1923), p. v.

11. Williams, *Beginnings of West Tennessee,* p. 51.

excellence. They seceded from their native grounds in Scotland and founded Ulster Plantation in northern Ireland. They seceded from this homeland and pushed to America, where they settled, separated, sought out and shaped new states—and continued their threats of secession. The aborted state of Franklin was a secession of those in the Watauga region from North Carolina in 1784. When botanist Andrew Michaux the younger was traveling through Tennessee in 1802, he believed that Tennessee would soon become two states. And during the ultimate secession of the Civil War, when Tennessee joined its adjoining southern states in sundering the Union, the state was continuously plagued by the threatened secession of its Unionist counties from the Confederacy.

Thus, protesting, separating, revolting, and believing, laboring, enduring, Tennesseans found and built their place. If their geography represented a wedding of opposites, so, too, did their character. Many of them were farmers who hated wars and suspected any standing army, but they did not shun a fight. Indeed, their vivid nickname—the Volunteers—reflects the readiness with which ordinary citizens rallied to the call to arms: with John Sevier at Kings Mountain, with "Old Hickory" at Horseshoe Bend and New Orleans, and in the Mexican War when 2,800 soldiers were requested by the national quota—and 30,000 Tennesseans offered to enlist.

Apparent contradictions in the character of Tennesseans were made manifest in the personality of its heroic prototype, Andrew Jackson. In their history, *Tennessee,* Folmsbee, Corlew, and Mitchell point out this complexity:

> James Parton, writing little more than a decade after Jackson's death, despaired at the conflicting sources which his research uncovered and concluded that his subject was both a patriot and a traitor. Old Hickory, wrote Parton, "was one of the greatest generals, and wholly ignorant of the art of war; . . . a writer brilliant, elegant, eloquent, without being able to compose a correct sentence, or spell words of four syllables. The first statesman, he never devised, he never framed a measure. He was the most candid of men, and was capable of the profoundest dissimulation. [He was] a most law-defying, law-obeying citizen. A stickler for discipline, he never

hesitated to disobey his superior. [He was] a democratic autocrat
. . . urbane savage . . . atrocious saint.'' [12]

Tennesseans have believed in the gun, the Bible, and themselves—not necessarily in that order, but all together.

The gun was an implement, first, of their survival and then of
their livelihood and then their justice. Its use had two highly
regarded virtues: it was personal, and it was swift. In their
religion, most of these people had rejected any intermediaries
between an individual and his God; it followed that they would
be unwilling to allow many mediators in a person's search for
justice.

Their initial effort at self-government in the Watauga Association explained that they did not want to become a shelter for
fleeing debtors or criminals seeking a haven. But if outlaws
such as the terrible Harpe brothers, who were judged to have
murdered some thirty innocent people in East Tennessee in the
last years of the eighteenth century, could not be brought down
by law, the people would do the job—and leave the head of at
least one of them impaled on a public stake to impart its silent,
grisly warning. It has been said of the early Tennessean that his
rifle, knife, and horse could all be turned to war at a moment's
notice. The Tennessean's reliance on his gun has persisted. One
observer describes his domain as ''the territory south of the
Smith and Wesson line.''

It has been said of the Scotch-Irish that they feared God—but
nothing else. They kept the Sabbath—and anything else they
could get their hands on.

They wanted to get their hands on—and in—the land. In their
passion for acquisition of land, they were in good company:
George Washington, the father of his country, and James Robertson, the father of the state, and a large assortment of other
surveyors, speculators, farmers, political leaders. If ''the activities of the early land companies were decisive factors in the colonization of the wilderness,'' as historian Archibald Henderson

---

12. Stanley J. Folmsbee, Robert E. Corlew, and Enoch L. Mitchell, *Tennessee: A
Short History* (Knoxville: University of Tennessee Press, 1969), p. 164.

asserts,[13] perhaps present land (and mineral) companies are decisive factors in a new "frontier" relationship today between human and natural resources.

Thus the land brings us full circle in the scope of this chapter, this book: back to the three grand divisions that are Tennessee. And the paradoxes that are the Tennessean.

He is the exuberant warrior, John Sevier, and the peace-seeking Secretary of State, Cordell Hull; he is Andrew Jackson, who opened the White House to Westerners, and Andrew Johnson, who sought to return Southerners there. He is democratic Davy Crockett, whose adversaries were not only bears and wild beasts but land speculators who threatened the small land-squatters he represented in Congress, and the land-greedy who pushed the Cherokees from their homeland. He is Casey Jones, who opened the throttle on his shiny locomotive and plunged into immortality; and newspaper giant Adolph S. Ochs, whose successful *Chattanooga Times* was ancestor to his *New York Times*. He is James K. Polk, eleventh president of the United States, who, in his successful race for the presidency in 1844, failed to carry his own ornery Tennessee, and he is Clarence Saunders, who had an early vision of the supermarket, made and lost a fortune in a chain he called Piggly Wiggly Stores, while engaging in a historic struggle with Wall Street power. He is the dedicated prohibitionist and the wily moonshiner co-existing in mutual success.

The Tennessean is Ann Robertson, sister of James, organizing a "bucket brigade" to pour scalding water on Indian attackers scaling the stockade at Fort Caswell on the Watauga; and she is Madam Annie of Memphis, who cared for yellow fever victims in her famous "house" until she, too, died in the epidemic. She is Rachel Jackson, frontier woman for all seasons, and runner Wilma Rudolph, who won three gold medals in the 1960 Olympic games. She is courageous actress Patricia Neal and popular singer Dinah Shore; and she is all the nameless midwives, schoolteachers, fetchers and carriers, crusaders

13. Archibald Henderson, *The Conquest of the Old Southwest* (New York: The Century Company, 1920), p. xv.

and civilizers whose names are forever lost, but whose gift is a steppingstone rather than a millstone for their fellow humans.

And Tennesseans are something more. They are red and black: one earliest and freest in this land, owning his place by right of prior claim and use and oneness with its creation; the other brought in bondage to this plot from halfway across the world and winning his place by right of toil and suffering and closeness to its earth, its rivers, its bounty, and its seasons.

These Tennesseans, too, are richly varied: quiet, scholarly Sequoyah, whose unique genius developed a Cherokee alphabet or syllabary and turned his people into a literate nation; and fierce Dragging Canoe, one of Tennessee's earliest secessionists, who separated himself from the treaty-makers among his people and led an implacable band of warriors, the Chickamaugas, in the Moccasin Bend country of the Tennessee River to contest every acre of their shrinking land. They are Nancy Ward, Beloved Woman and powerful leader among the Cherokees, friend to the earliest British settlers; and an unknown farmer, Tsali, who gave his life during the Cherokee removal so that a remnant of the great tribe could remain in their mountain homeland.

Two of Tennessee's most bitter tragedies involved these Tennesseans: the arrival of enslaved Africans and the removal of unwanted Indians. Each travail revealed the paradoxes of the predominant whites: in Andy Jackson, tough advocate of independence for most Americans, who favored forced Cherokee removal to the West, and in Davy Crockett, who opposed removal, voted against it, and lost his seat in Congress, whereupon he informed the voters of his state that they could go to hell, he was going to Texas. He did and died at the siege of the Alamo. And some 14,000 Cherokees followed the long Trail of Tears across the Mississippi to Oklahoma, at least a fourth of them finding graves beneath the snow and cold and driving rain of winter along the way.

Similar paradoxes existed in policies toward black Tennesseans. Four decades before the Civil War, in 1819, Elihu Embree began publishing the *Manumission Intelligencer* at Jonesboro, the state's oldest town. After a year, he changed the newspaper into a monthly, *The Emancipator*. These were the first antislavery journals in the nation. Shortly after the Civil War, at the town of Pulaski, the first klavern of the Ku Klux Klan had its murky birth. Emancipators and klansmen each found a following in Tennessee. And the Tennessean is also Will Handy, who made songs out of work and blues; he is a nameless black man who died aboard John Donelson's boat, *Adventure*, near the Suck of the Tennessee River; and he is humanistic sociologist, Charles S. Johnson.

The place and the people—varied, forever interacting.

The individualism of the frontier: independent and idealistic, relying on instinct more than introspection, combining intuition and initiative, alert to insult—real or implied. Tennessee has known many frontiers. Perhaps the first, the frontier of the unknown wilderness and its inhabitants, contained wisdom for later adventurers to recognize, speaking to America even today.

To the Cherokees who shaped a distinctive way of life in the eastern mountains and valleys of the Tennessee country, the world was bright with faith in the visible and shrouded with dread of the invisible. In a supplication of kinship similar to that voiced by St. Francis of Assisi, "Sun, my creator" was a recurring invocation in their prayers. But the dark mystery of death was personified in the dread Raven Mocker.

This wizard or witch, diving through the air on fiery wings with a hoarse cry, could enter a house all unseen and steal life from a dying person—unless turned aside by the power of a medicine man. A Raven Mocker could take the heart from a corpse and devour it and leave no scar. When other witches heard a Raven Mocker scream, they scattered like "pigeons when the hawk swoops."

The commonplace world of daily routine and familiar surroundings was also laden with magic. To the Cherokees, every living segment of the natural world around them harbored its own spirit. A mountain that appeared quite ordinary to the uninstructed observer might represent the enchanted abode of friends or hunters long since dead. A small, plain, spring lizard might possess the power to bring or withhold rain. A star was a bird with luminous feathers.

Giants and Little Folk dwelt in cliffs or woods or subterranean caves, harassing or helping their human neighbors. A tiny chickadee contained strange power to foretell arrival of a friend, while the ill omen of an owl's cry required a conjurer's skill and intercession. Nothing was too familiar or nondescript to escape attention and respect.

There was a deep difference between this ancient red inhabitor who had found his place within the complex natural world around him and the new white conqueror who would use and adapt that natural world, through his own inventiveness, to find *its* place in *his* scheme of things.

The difference was set forth with particular clarity by an early observer, who said he had reflected on the Indian's attitude regarding the relationship of man to other creatures.

> Although they consider themselves superior to all other animals and are very proud of that superiority; although they believe that the beasts of the forest, the birds of the air, and the fishes of the waters were created by the Almighty Being for the use of man; yet it seems as if they ascribe the difference between themselves and the brute kind, and the dominion which they have over them, more to their superior bodily strength and dexterity than to their immortal souls.[14]

Since all creation is interdependent, humans are "only the first among equals, the legitimate hereditary sovereigns of the whole animated race, of which they are themselves a constituent part." Thus, the Cherokee language did not contain genders of masculine and feminine, but instead genders of animate and inanimate. "Indeed, they go so far as to include trees, and plants within the first of these descriptions. All animated nature, in whatever degree, is in their eyes a great whole from which they have not yet ventured to separate themselves."[15]

A great whole.

This wholeness of the red person's vision was brought into abrupt confrontation with the white person's division. The newcomers from Europe looked upon the land and saw that it was good. They promptly set about dividing it into many parcels.

14. James Mooney, *Myths of the Cherokee,* American Indian History Series, 19th Annual Report of Bureau of American Ethnology (1900; reprint edition, St. Clair Shores, Michigan: Scholarly Press, 1970), p. 445.
    15. Mooney, *Myths of the Cherokee,* p. 445.

2

"The Kingdom of Paradise"

*T*HE western frontier which would eventually be known as Tennessee attracted them all: seekers after gold and glory; trappers of fur and dealers in raw, reeking, precious hides; builders of empire; dreamers of a better society wrought in this world and saviors of souls won for a next world; speculators making their own laws and rogues fleeing all law; and settlers—always the settlers—scrambling along the narrow trails, hacking out homesteads in the wilderness, clinging tenaciously, ferociously, to their newly won rights of property and liberty. They represented the great proud kingdoms of Europe.

The Spaniards came first.

A century and a third before any other Europeans, in 1540, Hernando de Soto, having honed his appetite and aptitude for conquest in the subjugation of Peru, led his retinue of cavalry and footmen, Spanish aristocrats and royal representatives and Indian burden bearers, into the interior of eastern North America, seeking gold and, incidentally, the Great River spoken of by native red men. Such a venture, penetrating an unmapped terrain of undefined dangers among unknown tribes, required a prodigal boldness blending equal portions of arrogance, courage, and greed.

While their route remains open to speculation, there is some agreement that de Soto's expedition touched Tennessee along the Hiwassee and Tennessee rivers in the east and then again in the vicinity of Memphis, where the Great River flowed. It was a route marked by blood and fire and treachery; it augured ill for the long history of red-white relations to follow.

Astride their horses, carrying muskets and crossbows, encased in armor tarnished with time and weather but still reflecting the brilliant summer sun, haughty in their superiority, bitter in their mounting disillusionment with the long, unproductive search, the Spaniards persisted. They found yellow metal—and it turned out to be copper. Pearls from the coast were hoarded—and lost along the way. Cherokee women and children fled the intruders, whose ugly reputation for kidnapping and enslavement preceded them. Finally, they arrived in the country of the Chickasaws—northern Mississippi and adjacent portions of Alabama and Tennessee—and the mighty waters that had been their destination. De Soto's meticulous and faithful secretary, Rangel, described the final despair of that first tourist's exploitive journey:

> I saw Don Antonio Osorio, brother to the Lord Marquis of Astorgas, wearing a short garment of the blankets of that country, torn on the sides, his flesh showing. No hat, barefooted, without hose or shoes, a buckler on his back, a sword without a shield; midst heavy frosts and cold. And the stuff of which he was made, and his illustrious lineage, made him endure his toil without lament such as many others made; for there was no one who could help him although he was the man he was, and had in Spain two thousand ducats of income from the church. And the day this gentleman saw him, he did not believe he had eaten a mouthful, and he had to dig for it with his nails to get something to eat. . . .
>
> Onward to his grave in the great river which he was to discover, marched the conquistador, Hernando de Soto, until, on the banks of the Father of Waters, "finding all things against him, he sickened and died." [1]

Frenchmen were next to see the Chickasaw Bluffs where an expanding city named Memphis would one day stand. The year

1. John P. Brown, *Old Frontiers: The Story of the Cherokee Indians from the Earliest Times to the Date of Their Removal to the West, 1838,* First American Frontier Series (1938; reprint edition, New York: Arno Press, 1971), p. 39.

was 1673. Representing the two forces that would dominate French influence throughout the vast interior region of America were a fur trader, Louis Jolliet of Quebec, and a missionary, Father Jacques Marquette.

Alert, observant, surrounded by the luxuriant world of late June and early July along the fertile river banks, Jolliet and Marquette found their way down the Mississippi in birch canoes. They noted rich veins of iron, thick canebrakes, troublesome "musquitoes," and increasing stands of elm, and cypress trees, which they found magnificent in size and height. An encounter with Indians revealed that red man and white were about equally frightened of each other. An invitation to eat resulted in the Europeans feasting on buffalo meat and wild plums. Their response to the country and its natives suggested the powerful influence that the French would exert on development of Tennessee and the surrounding area.

For decades, more than a century since the first Spanish thrust inland, there had been no European visitor to the area and now, in the space of a month—July 1673—there were approaches from the two extremities. For while the French Jesuit, Marquette, and the trader, Jolliet, were examining the banks along the Mississippi, two Englishmen, James Needham and Gabriel Arthur, were glimpsing the great Valley of the Tennessee as they ventured across the Alleghenies. Sent on their exploration by enterprising Abraham Wood, owner of a Virginia trading post deep in the hinterlands, these two found, during their two journeys into the back country, a paradoxical range of experience—from murder to friendship—that would characterize generations of English-Cherokee relations.

James Needham was a successful young planter only recently arrived from England. Gabriel Arthur was probably trader Wood's indentured servant. Accompanied by eight Indians, they were the first Englishmen to enter the Overhill Cherokee country.

After initial success, one of those very guides—Indian John—hired for "protection and safety," became disaffected and, according to the account left by Abraham Wood, based on Arthur's recollections, "catched up a gunn, which hee him selfe had carried to kill meat for them to eate and shot Mr. Needham neare ye burr of ye eare and killd him.'' With warm praise tempered by cool realism, Wood concluded: ''So died this heroyick English man whose fame shall never die if my penn were able to eternize it which had adventured where never any English man had dared to atempt before and with him died one hundered forty-foure pounds starling of my adventure with him.'' [2]

Blood and pounds sterling would continue as the basic currency feeding frontier exploration. Now, however, Needham was dead and Arthur was threatened with burning at the stake. He was spared and gradually won favor with his captors. He accompanied them on war trips and on hunts and became familiar with much of the terrain and many of the Indians' customs before he returned to Abraham Wood's post in June 1674, bringing his tale of murder and loss along with his account of knowledge gained first-hand.

Spanish. French. English. Gradually, they were beginning the jostle, the squeeze and positioning for influence that would accelerate and intensify until at last it became the struggle using Indians and many of their European counterparts as living pawns in a giant power play whose stakes were life and death and the future of a continent.

From this moment on, like water wearing away a mountain, each new contact between red man and white opened a new trickle of ideas and future possibilities, encouraging a gradual flood of changes, and, eventually, the destructive hurricane itself. Among those who poured into the mountainous Tennessee country of the Overhill Cherokee during these early years— seeking fortune, anonymity, knowledge, excitement—certain personalities emerge with particular force, foreshadowing future arrivals and choices. Each responded to his own frontier as presented by the forbidding, beckoning wilderness.

One of the earliest and most incredible of these visitors was Sir Alexander Cuming, a self-appointed ambassador of good will from the King of England to such Cherokee royalty as could be discovered. When nothing more grandiose than a prin-

2. Williams, *Early Travels,* p. 21.

cipal chief could be found to exist among the Cherokees, Cuming promptly remedied the deficiency by designating him Emperor Moytoy of Tellico.

Bold and imaginative, Sir Alexander Cuming was the sort of
man whose debits and dreams consistently outdistance his income and realities. When he arrived in Charles Town, in December 1729, Sir Alexander was thirty-eight years old, brilliant
and charming, at the pinnacle of his persuasive talents and his
hopes for an eventual royal commission. For their part, the
Cherokees were deeply dissatisfied in their English alliances and
were contemplating joining the Creeks in vows of friendship
with the French. Circumstances were ripe for the decisive role
played by peripatetic, flamboyant, half-mad, half-prophetic Sir
Alexander in securing Cherokee ties with the English and determining the immediate course of Tennessee's frontier history.

A forerunner of many such ambivalent characters to come,
Sir Alexander Cuming, a Scottish baronet trained in law, was
both an ambassador—without portfolio—and an entrepreneur—without visible resources. He was familiar with the New
World through his aspiration to be made governor of the Ber-
muda Islands, and he was acquainted with the wiles of high finance through investigation of the famous South Sea Company
Bubble which had ruined hundreds of British family fortunes.

To government officials, to prospering tradesmen and professionals, and to the planters enjoying profits of their rich acres,
the confident Cuming represented himself as master of a great
estate back in the Isles who was now ready to establish its counterpart in South Carolina. The promissory notes he issued lav-
ishly were promptly redeemed whenever a creditor presented
them for payment, and in a short while the Cuming notes carried all the authority of colonial currency. They circulated
freely.

Early on, negotiations for his purchase of several plantations
were begun. On one of these he built a bastion called the Treasury, of stone, boasting walls three feet thick with stout doors
and windows. The loan office he established multiplied its
flourishing business. Notes were issued at ten percent interest,
for which his borrowers mortgaged their homes and plantations

to him. On this security, he bought quantities of gold and silver and shipments of the colony's produce, which he sent out from the busy Charles Town port. Undoubtedly, the rich trade in pelts, especially in the thousands of deerskins brought down each year from the Cherokee hunting grounds, captured his alert attention, while the immense brooding land at the very back door of this colony stirred his imagination—one asset Sir Alexander possessed in abundance.

By spring of 1730, he had determined to lay aside, momentarily, his entrepreneur's role and develop his potential as ambassador for King George II and British authority. Accompanied by several influential leaders from the Carolina colony and a number of the oldest Indian traders in the business—including as interpreter Eleazar Wiggan, the "Old Rabbit," who had been trading for almost twenty years with the Indians—Sir Alexander Cuming set forth into the wilderness in mid-March.

Ten days and some three hundred miles later, Sir Alexander arrived at the town of Keowee in the Lower Cherokee settlements. Rumors of a surly suspicion festering among these towns had made even the traders reluctant to visit Keowee. But Sir Alexander, fortified with three cases of pistols, as well as a sword under his greatcoat, despite warnings that the Indians never came armed to their council, presented himself at the Town-House.

There in the flickering firelight, impressed by this stranger's boldness and eloquence, more than three hundred Indians bent their knees in allegiance to His Majesty King George's sovereignty.

The triumphal tour continued through the Middle Cherokee settlements and finally crossed the mountains into the Overhill country and the present boundaries of Tennessee. Here lived Moytoy of Tellico, principal chief over all the other chiefs of the Cherokee towns. At Tellico and Nequassee, there were ceremonies that culminated on April 3. Sir Alexander recorded the event in his Journal:

> This was a Day of Solemnity, the greatest that ever was seen in the Country; there was Singing, Dancing, Feasting, making of Speeches, the Creation of Moytoy Emperor, with the unanimous

Consent of all the head Men assembled from the different Towns of the Nation, a Declaration of their resigning their Crown, Eagles Tails, Scalps of their Enemies, as an Emblem of their all owning His Majesty King George's Sovereignty over them . . . the Declaration of Obedience was made on their Knees.[3]

Sir Alexander climaxed this achievement with the boldest of all his inspirations. He invited a delegation of the Cherokees to accompany him to England and the royal court.

Emperor Moytoy declined the hospitality because his wife was ill. But after some deliberation, seven leaders accepted the invitation. In this delegation was a young warrior whose presence gave the journey significance far beyond the picturesque moment. His name was (or would become, in later maturity) Attakullakulla, or Little Carpenter, and he was destined to be, in the opinion of some historians, the greatest of Cherokee statesmen. His experience in England remained a decisive factor in his lifelong friendship for British interests.

The group departed Charles Town aboard a man-of-war, the *Fox,* in May, the first Cherokees to cross the Atlantic, and arrived at Dover in June. In London, these early red Tennesseans dined with the King, were dazzled by the magnificent surroundings, sat for a group portrait by the great painter Hogarth (done, alas, with the Cherokees camouflaged in British court garb rather than their own unique dress). Articles of agreement between the two peoples were drawn up and gravely signed. Peace and friendship was promised "as long as the Mountains and Rivers shall last, or the Sun shine." It was a pretty pledge that would be repeated in many treaties yet to be written—both its freshness and truth fading with the years.

The lionizing of the Cherokees continued—at fairs and dinners and regimental drills, at the theater, at archery contests. One of the Indian princes was rumored engaged to "a young lady of French extraction." The King could not remember when he had been better diverted than by acquaintance with the Indian visitors. They stayed for four months and departed without their friend.

3. Williams, *Early Travels,* p. 136.

Sir Alexander Cuming did not feel it would be healthy for him to return to Charles Town. Shortly after he had left the colony aboard the *Fox,* one of his numerous notes had been protested. Suspicion led to action, and the Treasury stronghold on his plantation was broken open. Its stout walls guarded only empty boxes and rubbish. In a letter from South Carolina to Edinburgh, one of the disillusioned Carolinians observed wryly, "We have only this comfort left for the Loss of our Money, that no Man can laugh at his Neighbours; or rather, that every Man may laugh at all his Neighbours." [4]

Sir Alexander had both swindled and served the English Carolinians. His grandiose financial empire crumbled without a trace. But his remarkable diplomatic jaunt into the back country and the visit of his Indian friends in London resulting in a remarkable treaty marked a watershed in Cherokee-British relations. The Cherokee would, in the future, take up the war-hatchet against the British, but there would be one consistent Peace Chief, Attakullakulla, the Little Carpenter, ever ready to renew efforts of friendship as he recalled the faraway country and the energetic, enigmatic charmer who had conducted him there.

Another distinctive personality who appeared in the Overhill country in these early days was indeed a rarity—an adventurer who sought neither financial gain nor diplomatic advantage for any European power. He was that most dangerous of all threats to the Establishment, an adventurer in ideas.

Christian Gottlieb Priber arrived in the Tennessee country in 1736, six years after Sir Alexander Cuming. A scholar-dreamer, neither imposing in stature nor impressive in appearance, this highly educated master of seven languages had left a wife and four children in Saxony to form a radically new system of government in a new land. Passing through Charles Town with only a ripple of response, Priber stopped briefly at a township farther inland, then made his way to the country of the Overhill Cherokee. There, at Great Tellico, he exchanged his continental clothing for breechclout and moccasins and unpacked the tools of his

---

4. Williams, *Early Travels,* p. 118.

trade, the weapons of his attack: his books. With books and pen
and paper he would send tremors of dismay through the colonial
establishment and challenge basic British assumptions regarding
government.

Rumors seeped down to Charles Town from the Cherokee
country that subversive ideas were circulating through the Overhill towns. Discontent was stirring. There was a deepening
sense of power and self-reliance that fostered neutrality toward all European alliances. Such a development could mean
only one thing to the official British mind: a French agent at
work. When traders' accounts began to include some of the
ideas the strange German scholar was sowing among the Indians, the supposition grew, later accepted by many historians,
that Priber was a Jesuit priest sent on his mission by French
authorities.

Actually, French authority would have reacted with no less
alarm than the English, had it been as directly challenged by
Christian Priber's influence—for what Priber proposed was a
balance of power, with the Cherokees holding the scales in their
own territory, using their own military prowess and strategic situation for their own advantage. To those who saw native peoples only as pawns in "civilized" nations' struggles, such a
proposal was heresy. They looked for other motives behind the
selfless preachments of autonomy and independence.

There *was* another purpose motivating Priber. His dream was
nothing less than a new nation, a more perfect society, a republic to be called the Kingdom of Paradise. Its broad outlines suggested those goals set forth by numerous experiments in an ideal
communism: liberty and law equally enjoyed and administered,
and a just balance between every citizen's needs and every person's contributions. From each according to his talents, to each
according to his needs: this was Christian Priber's goal.

When a young French captive, Antoine Bonnefoy, was
brought to Great Tellico by the Cherokees in 1742, he was
amazed to find there a scholarly German dressed as an Indian
who sought his support for a projected Kingdom of Paradise.
During long discussions, Bonnefoy learned details of Priber's
republic, which he recorded in a journal. Trade was to be open

with both French and English; there would be no superiority, but perfect equality; all goods would be held in common; each person would work according to his talents for the good of the republic; women would have the same freedom as men; there would be no marriage contract, and children would belong to the republic.

Priber's own exception to the rules of common ownership revealed that fatal flaw common to many such paradises: each person had his own version of the "exceptions." For Christian Priber, in Paradise, the individual's only property would be books and paper and ink. These happened to be the very items Priber needed in his own work.

Preparatory to establishing his ideal nation in the Overhill country, Priber reshaped the government of Great Tellico. When the chief medicine man was crowned emperor, surrounded by a court bearing appropriate titles, Priber became secretary of state. When Governor Glen in Charles Town received letters signed by the new bearer of this title, he decided that this troublesome situation had developed far enough. Ludovick Grant, the trusty Scotch trader on whom Charles Town officials relied for authentic information about the back country, was sent to Great Tellico to arrest Priber and bring him before the colony's authorities.

Grant returned alone. He had gone to Great Tellico and into the very Town-House to arrest Priber, only to find that gentleman already aware of his plans. Surrounded by friends, Priber challenged the trader to lay a hand on him—and then laughed at Grant's frustration. Such insolence was intolerable to Ludovick Grant.

The governor shared his trader's outrage. The situation called for military muscle. Colonel Fox was commissioned to proceed at once up to the mountains to take Mr. Priber into custody as an enemy to the public repose.

The colonel's first strategy was to try to lure Priber out of Great Tellico and the protection of his red brothers. He did not succeed. Then the colonel proceeded to the great square, where affairs of state were decided, and tried to seize the odd little German. This failed so ignominiously that finally the colonel was happy to forget his mission and depart with his scalp intact and a verbal passport of safe conduct from the Secretary of State himself. Then Priber resumed work on his compilation of notes about the Cherokees and the dictionary of their language that he hoped to have published in Paris.

All went well until the summer of 1743. Conditions seemed ripe for an enlargement of the Kingdom of Paradise. With a small group of Indian friends, Priber set out on a journey to French Fort Toulouse in the Alabama country. En route, the party was attacked by Creek Indians, directed and aided by English traders, and Christian Priber was captured. He was taken as far from the Overhill country as possible, to Frederica on the Georgia coast. Imprisoned in the fort there, Priber continued to promote the idea of his Paradise and to work on the manuscript he carried with him at the time of his capture.

Christian Priber died in Fort Frederica prison. His dream of Paradise died with him. His writing and papers disappeared forever. The Overhill Cherokee towns reassured the English traders of their friendship—all except Great Tellico. For years, its people remembered the message that their scholarly, idealistic Prime Minister Priber had brought them—and they refused exclusive English rights to their friendship.

Such independence won the hostility of that varied, sometimes villainous, sometimes helpful, often greedy group, the traders. They had been among the earliest Europeans to come into the Tennessee country in significant numbers, forming a necessary link between the Indian nations, the colonial governments, and the London merchants. In the early days, each trader received a license to serve two towns. He lived a large part of each year among the Indians, frequently had an Indian wife and children, and advanced supplies on credit against the skins he would take by pack-horse to the Charles Town dealers, who shipped them to the London merchants who had put up the initial stock of goods. Such goods included guns, powder, lead and flints, clothing, knives, blankets, scissors, salt, tea, kettles, and numerous similar items—especially looking glasses for the warriors. The Indian trade was built on a chain of credit; fortunes were made—by the London and Charles Town merchants;

traders and their red customers were less fortunate. Thousands of deerskins and other pelts taken out of the wilderness each year brought all too meager returns of things that would rust, wear out, break, or be used up within a short time.

The quality and nature of the goods was a continuing bone of contention. Such simple articles were, indeed, tokens of the first real Tennessee frontier. For if the Sir Alexander Cumings and the Christian Pribers represented early frontiers of diplomacy and Utopian dreams, the trader with the Indians introduced another element into the frontier: products, goods, things, objects invented and manufactured and used by men—things whetting new appetites, creating something called "markets." And in the ultimate paradox, while the trader created the passion for the fruits of the white man's civilization, he also introduced the means for repelling the further advance of that civilization. The ambivalence was between the Cherokees' desire for goods and guns and involved their devotion to that land which was the major resource they could exchange for the white man's wares. The dilemma was expressed by the Chief Oconostota, when he said, "I will sell them the land, but a few presents are as nothing compared to good land, which will last forever." Those early traders who stimulated a hunger for manufactured goods were harbingers of that which was shoddy and that which was worthy in the commerce to develop during two centuries to follow.

The early trader in the Tennessee country led a harsh, lonely, tenacious life. His pack-train of a dozen or more animals bore heavy burdens along meandering buffalo trails, the bells ringing, tinkling, clanging around their necks, vying with the whoops and shouts of impatient drivers. As his appetite for profits grew, the quality of the trader's goods often diminished. His widening margin of profit squeezed the Indians. Many traders disregarded laws prohibiting sale of rum. Their reputation declined, and when Lt. Gov. Robert Dinwiddie of Virginia called them "abandoned wretches," he was reflecting a generally accepted opinion.

Edmond Atkin, a London-born Charles Town merchant engaged in the Indian trade, reported to the Board of Trade in

London that unscrupulous traders in rum would often place themselves along the paths followed by hunters returning home with their deerskins. The Indians "when Drunk are easily cheated. After parting with the fruit of three or four Months Toil, they find themselves at home, without the means of buying the necessary Clothing for themselves or their families. Their Domestick and inward Quiet being broke, reflection sours them, and disposes them for Mischief. To the same cause is owing, that the Quality of their Leather is Debased. For those Rum Traders take any Skins, badly dressed, and untrimmed; which require one Horse the more in 5 or 6 to carry them, and harbour Worms that daily destroy them. And the Indians require the other Traders in their Towns to take them in the same Condition. . . . a licentiousness hath crept in among the young men, beyond the Power of the Head Men to remedy." [5]

This was the worst aspect of the Indian trade. One of its better representatives in the Tennessee country was the unusual—indeed, unique—James Adair. Scotch-Irish, well-educated, blending the spirited curiosity of the student and artist with the practical acquisitiveness of commerce, Adair appeared in the Tennessee area of the Overhill Cherokees the same year as Christian Priber, 1736. The contrast between the two men was significant.

James Adair came as a trader. But he became much more: a diplomat and even, on occasion, a fellow warrior, strengthening ties to England rather than France; a philosopher expounding the theory of Indian descent from the Lost Tribes of Israel; and most important, a historian, whose work, *A History of the American Indians,* published in London in 1775, provides one of the few records of an early and obscure period in the manners and customs of the Southern Indians. With all its peculiarities and prejudices, the book remains fascinating today, revealing a great deal about the life of the Cherokees in those towns along the Little Tennessee River and its tributaries, and especially

5. Edmond Atkin, *The Appalachian Indian Frontier: The Edmond Atkin Report and Plan of 1755,* edited by Wilbur R. Jacobs. (Lincoln: University of Nebraska Press, 1967), p. 35.

about the "cheerful brave Chikkasah" among whom Adair was especially happy.

Adair has been described as "the forest student, traversing the toilsome trail to Charles Town with peltry to trade for books" and as the rollicking companion to "an illiterate and coarse-grained white man, the two riding carelessly along a dangerous path, singing as they went, each braced by 'a hearty draught of punch,' and further companioned by a keg of rum. Wherever and however seen, his was an unusual figure, riding, we may be sure, a coveted Chickasaw steed through vast forest reaches, silhouetted against a background of forest-green. Whether knight-errant or dare-devil, or a commingling of both, he rode into mundane immortality." [6]

Adair's literary ventures were in part a response to commercial controversies in which he became embroiled, especially over trade licenses with the Choctaws, another of the great Southern tribes he visited during his more than forty years in the Indian country. Adair shared the opinion of his fellow Europeans that the most enterprising among themselves should have every claim to the resources of the Indian country. Apportioning access to those resources became more important than redeeming good faith between red people and white. But along the way, James Adair compiled one of the earliest and most fascinating records of little-known aspects of Tennessee's history.

Unfortunately, peace on the frontier did not always depend on individual attitudes and associations. One person, red or white, through lack of judgment or outright brutality could ignite hostilities that involved entire villages over long periods of time. On the other hand, one person acting as peacemaker could achieve only the most fragile victory. This contrast was due, in large part, to the fact that two powerful European countries were playing out some of their international struggle for dominance on this improbable stage. The struggle erupted in 1754 into the French and Indian War in America.

The Chickasaw tribe, influencing West Tennessee, had been

6. Samuel Cole Williams, editor, *Adair's History of the American Indians* (1930; reprint edition, Chicago: Swallow Press, Inc., 1973), pp. xx, xxi.

and remained unyielding foes of the French, although their power diminished following a defeat in 1739 by 3,600 Frenchmen and their Indian allies who rendezvoused at the Bluff where Memphis would one day stand.

The Cherokees were much less predictable. Sir Alexander Cuming's influence remained potent through the peace chief, Attakullakulla. But Christian Priber's warnings and exhortations echoed in the reluctance of Great Tellico and other villages to pledge full alliance with the British. Suspicion on both sides made the Cherokees and the British hesitant allies.

There was, for instance, the scourge of smallpox. It came among the Overhill Cherokees along with all the white men's gifts and goods that glittered so enticingly. The English traders explained that the germs of the terrible epidemic of 1738, in which perhaps half of the Cherokee Nation perished, arrived in Charles Town with a shipment of "Guinea-men," or African slaves, and were innocently transported to Indian country. But French agents whispered that the traders' goods had been purposely infected. Whenever the war chief, Oconostota, a proud, handsome man whose face was left pitted and ugly by smallpox, looked into the mirror, his rage against the British flared. In tribal councils, he became a French advocate and counterpoint to Attakullakulla.

With the outbreak of war in 1754, Lt. Col. George Washington voiced a general prediction that the French and Indian War could not be won by the English without the help of the Indians. Several years earlier, there had been a request by the Cherokees for a fort in the Overhill country to protect women and children when their warriors were away fighting the Shawnees and other Indian allies of the French. Not until actual hostilities had begun, however—in fact, while General Braddock was meeting defeat and death at Fort Duquesne—did South Carolina Governor Glen listen to a Cherokee delegation and give his promise to construct a strong fort. In exchange, the English would be given sovereignty over some forty million acres of plantation land.

Delays alternated with misunderstandings before Fort Loudoun on the Little Tennessee River was finally begun in 1756, the western-most English fort in America. Its brief, embattled existence would reflect in microcosm many of the personal quarrels, official errors of judgment and failures of leadership that would plague other Western forts during years to come when Americans were accelerating their irresistible push across the continent.

Construction of the fort, involving a small United Nations of talent and cross-purposes, was erratic. The remarkable feat may have been that it was eventually completed at all. The first controversy involved location.

John William Gerard de Brahm, German soldier by chance, engineer by profession, and alchemist by repute, who had reconstructed the fortifications of Charles Town, was assigned to lay out and build the fort. Captain Raymond Demere, "an officer of winning personality" who had previously served both in Georgia and Florida, was placed in charge of His Majesty's Independent Company of Charles Town, 200 men, to garrison the fort. When de Brahm was taken to the site chosen by the Indians, on the south side of the river between two hills, he disapproved. Impatiently, he demonstrated the dangers of this place, pointing out that the very shoe buckles the men wore could reflect light and be seen from either of the mountains. De Brahm selected a site farther down the river, more easily fortified. But the Indians protested that there was no level ground there for planting corn and vegetables. When Captain Demere informed de Brahm of the Indians' objections, he was startled by the engineer's response. De Brahm drew one of his pistols and offered it to the captain with instructions to shoot him through the head. When the chiefs Old Hop and Attakullakulla witnessed this extravagant reaction, they became even more unwilling to follow de Brahm's advice, and the original site was finally agreed upon. Demere was pleased with the 700-acre location, which he found pleasant and agreeable.

Work began promptly. Indians from nearby villages brought food by river and land. A bustling atmosphere of markets and construction prevailed. De Brahm remained quarrelsome, however, and persisted in disputing authority with the military officers on duty. Finally, in the bleak chill of late December, he abruptly departed. Old Hop christened him "the warrior who ran away in the night." Raymond Demere was furious when he wrote to the governor: "We are no engineers but will do our best for the Fort which scarce deserves the name of a camp. The Indians call it the Fort to keep horses and cows in." [7]

By early summer, 1757, this fort was more than a cow-lot, however. It stood near the fork of the Little Tennessee and Tellico rivers.

> The site was cleared of timber within the enclosure and for a distance of a rifle shot without it. A well was dug in the enclosure and walled up. A deep defensive ditch was dug; the plan called for the planting of a hedge of thorny locusts in its bottom to "render the fort impregnable at least against Indians who always engage naked." . . . The fort was securely built of heavy logs, square in shape, with blockhouses and bastions connected by palisades which were trunks of trees embedded in the earth touching each other, and sharpened at the top, with loopholes at proper places.
>
> The bastions were named in honor of members of the British royal family: A the King's; B the Duke of Cumberland's; C the Queen's, and D the Prince of Wales'. Stone was used in the fireplaces and chimneys.
>
> The fort, even before it was completed, was named in honor of John, Earl of Loudoun, who had recently arrived in America to take command of all British forces on the continent.
>
> Around the fort there gathered a few settlers, mostly traders, artisans and truck-raisers. Gunsmiths and blacksmiths were welcomed by the Indians who availed themselves of their skills. Some of the white men brought their wives, and the chatter and laughter of children of the English-speaking race were for the first time heard in the Tennessee country.[8]

The twelve cannon provided for defense of the fort were brought from Fort Prince George in the Lower Cherokee country. Their transport over the rough, narrow mountain trails was hazardous. According to de Brahm, the trader engaged to carry out the task

---

7. Brown, *Old Frontiers*, p. 73.

8. Samuel Cole Williams, *Dawn of the Tennessee Valley* (Johnson City, Tenn.: Watauga, 1937), p. 193.

contrived to poise on each horse a canon cross ways over the pack saddle, and lashed them round the horse's body with belts; but as these horses had to cross a country full of high mountains, and these covered with forrests, it would happen that sometimes one end of a canon would catch a tree, twist upon the saddle and draw the horse down, some of which had by these accidences their backs broken under the wight, and lost their lifs; the longest journey those horses could make was six miles a day.[9]

The Indians were impressed by such loud-speaking weapons as the cannon. The French, too, apparently took note, for their expected attack did not materialize. On August 14, Capt. Raymond Demere, who had not been well since his first arrival in the Cherokee country, turned over command of the fort and its garrison to his brother, Capt. Paul Demere. When the two brothers parted, there in the deep wilderness of the Tennessee country, they could not have guessed that they would never meet again.

For despite an interval of apparent quiet within the vicinity of the fort, continued French influence and a sequence of small conflicts between Indians and whites were gathering toward a storm that finally broke around Fort Loudoun in March 1760. The Cherokee emperor, Old Hop, had died and was replaced by the more truculent Standing Turkey, who now directed an attack against the fort. Attakullakulla remained peace chief and loyal to the whites, but his influence had vanished for the moment, and he withdrew into the forest with his family. The fort, which was originally intended to satisfy Cherokee demands for protection, then found itself under siege and needing protection from the Cherokees.

South Carolina appealed for aid from its neighbors, North Carolina and Virginia, and from the commander of the entire British force in America, Major General Jeffrey Amherst. Amherst sent one of his colonels and 1300 men to chastise the Indians and return to New York.

The Colonel and his men arrived in the South and proceeded

9. Williams, *Early Travels,* p. 192.

to lay waste and burn the towns of the Lower Cherokee. Then they encountered, in the Middle Towns, an ambush that was bloody and cost them several lives. Announcing that he had fulfilled his orders "to chastise," the Colonel hastily followed the order to return to New York. Fort Loudoun's fate was sealed.

For Capt. Paul Demere and his companions, both food and hope were in short supply. Indian wives of some of the soldiers slipped corn to them, but by summer the garrison was reduced to eating horse-flesh. Desertions increased as some of the men fled to the woods and threw themselves on the mercy of the Indians. Sickly, weak, despairing of rescue, Demere and his garrison capitulated on August 7.

Terms of agreement provided that the soldiers should march out of the fort with drums and arms and such powder and ball and baggage as was deemed necessary; with an Indian escort they would proceed unmolested to Virginia or Fort Prince George; the sick and lame should be cared for in the Indian towns; and "the fort, great guns, powder, ball, and spare arms, be delivered to the Indians without any fraud or further delay on the day appointed for the march of the Troops." [10]

On August 9, the English flag was struck and 180 men, 60 women, and a few children marched out of Fort Loudoun. There was no concern now whether the great wooden gate leading to the river hung ajar. There was no need now to check the palisades to see that they were sturdy. Behind the weary little group lay the pitiful fort that had been England's first official bastion in the Tennessee country. Ahead of them stretched the 140-mile march to Fort Prince George.

On the first day, they covered some fifteen miles. As they made camp, foreboding grew when the Indians who were escorting them gradually disappeared into the dusk. The next morning, as the apprehensive travelers prepared to move on, there was a volley of gunfire from ambush. A lieutenant returned the fire. With war cries and shouts, some 700 Indians

---

10. J. G. M. Ramsey, *The Annals of Tennessee to the End of the Eighteenth Century,* First American Frontier Series (1853; reprint edition, New York: Arno Press, 1971), p. 57.

emerged from the woods. Captain Demere, three other officers, twenty-three privates, and three women were killed before the day's terror ended. Of those remaining, some 120 were taken prisoner.

Paul Demere's death was slow and brutal. Wounded, scalped alive, he danced for his captors before both arms and legs were cut off. Stuffing his mouth with dirt, the Indians chanted, "You want land, we will give it to you."

Fate of some of the prisoners was also harsh, but only one other was tortured to death. Eventually, the remainder returned to South Carolina. One, Capt. John Stuart, was saved—at great risk and personal cost—by Attakullakulla himself.

Why had there been such total disregard of the agreement between the Indians and whites? The Cherokees said that when they searched Fort Loudoun after the garrison left, they found quantities of powder and ball that had been hidden by Captain Demere, contrary to his agreement to surrender all ammunition "without fraud." This deception had inflamed the young warriors and made it impossible to hold them to their part of the treaty assuring the whites safe withdrawal unmolested.

Fort Loudoun had fallen, but its presence in the Overhill country at a crucial moment of international conflict had helped assure British control of the western frontier.

And that same year, another significant event occurred, quietly. A long hunter who was also an explorer and settler penetrated to the northeastern area of the present Tennessee. Near a tributary of the Watauga River on the creek that would eventually bear his name, the restless adventurer carved his memento on a tree-trunk: "D. Boone cilled a bar on tree in the year 1760."

Within fifteen years, Fort Loudoun would be cruelly avenged, settlement would be trickling and then flooding across the mountains into Tennessee, and a momentous treaty would be arranged in large part by Daniel Boone.

The vengeance: When General Amherst heard of the fall of Fort Loudoun, he wrote of his shame at this first instance of His Majesty's troops having yielded before the Indians. To lessen his humiliation, the general dispatched Col. James Grant on a

Cherokee expedition. Colonel Grant immediately realized that the war was unnecessary but he found peace to be an unpopular idea. Popular opinion won out over common sense, and Grant launched a campaign that could bring everyone shame. The nature of the 1761 destruction of Lower Cherokee towns is suggested by a description of one of Grant's lieutenants, Francis Marion, who would soon become famous as a Revolutionary War leader, nicknamed the Swamp Fox. He wrote:

> We proceeded, by Colonel Grant's orders, to burn the Indian cabins. Some of the men seemed to enjoy this cruel work, laughing heartily at the curling flames, but to me it appeared a shocking sight. Poor creatures, thought I, we surely need not grudge you such miserable habitations. But when we came, according to orders, to cut down the fields of corn, I could scarcely refrain from tears. Who, without grief, could see the stately stalks with broad green leaves and tasseled shocks, the staff of life, sink under our swords with all their precious load, to wither and rot untasted in their mourning fields.[11]

The settlement: Everyone on the western frontier had suffered during the harsh French and Indian War. By the Treaty of Paris, signed in February 1763, all of North America east of the Mississippi was made a British possession. The long contest between French and British was resolved. Settlers and speculators pushed from Virginia, North Carolina, and Pennsylvania to make the first permanent homes in East Tennessee's valleys and hills. There was William Bean on the Watauga branch of the Holston River, whose son, Russell, was the first white child born west of the Alleghenies; and John Carter in Carter's Valley; and Jacob Brown on the Nolichucky River. And by 1772, there was a Watauga Association of settlers along the Watauga and Nolichucky Rivers who felt that, being outside the protective bounds of Virginia or North Carolina, they needed to form some government of their own. The result, "a purely democratic government," set both the spirit and reality of later political organizations and institutions that would arise in Tennessee.

11. Brown, *Old Frontiers,* p. 111.

The treaty: These settlers occupied lands they did not own, but merely leased from the Indians. When Judge Richard Henderson of North Carolina, representing his Transylvania Company, a gigantic land speculation enterprise, aided by the advice and efforts of Daniel Boone, met some 1,200 Cherokees at Sycamore Shoals of the Watauga River in March 1775, the settlers in the region also attended the conference. After three days of negotiation between the most powerful chiefs of the Cherokee and leaders of the transmontane frontier, a treaty was signed which heralded "the opening of the West." Some twenty million acres—the Tennessee country drained by the Cumberland River and all its tributaries, and almost all the present state of Kentucky—was purchased from the Cherokees by the Transylvania Company for ten thousand pounds' worth of goods. Jacob Brown and John Carter and the Wataugans promptly negotiated to buy their land, as well. Such purchase was prohibited by British law, but the small homesteader was merely following the example (and success) of the big speculator. And before this decisive treaty had even been signed, Daniel Boone and a party of hardy woodsmen were already on their way to blaze a path by which the civilization Boone so desperately shunned could come to possess the wilderness he so fervently cherished.

The 1775 Treaty of Sycamore Shoals marked an end and a beginning. The influence of Attakullakulla, of European visionaries and English diplomats and governors and generals was waning. Their places would be taken by homegrown frontier fighter-statesmen who wanted to be free of all European ties. Two men in particular personified the spirit of these two groups: Dragging Canoe, fierce, eloquent, charismatic Cherokee; and John Sevier, fierce, eloquent, charismatic frontiersman. Each of these would lead a secession movement that changed the history of his people.

At Sycamore Shoals, the tall, pockmarked Dragging Canoe stood before his slight, aging, revered father, Attakullakulla, and the other leaders of his people, and forcefully protested further loss of Cherokee land which was melting away "like balls of snow in the sun." He opposed his father and pleaded for resistance to the cabin choked full of trader's goods that was to be their payment. But speculator Richard Henderson won possession to the vast tract of Cherokee land. Three days of debate and deliberation culminated in a solemn treaty—and in one of the famous prophecies of American history, as Dragging Canoe confronted the triumphant Henderson and passionately divined the future: "You have bought a fair land, but there is a cloud hanging over it. You will find its settlement dark and bloody."

The years immediately ahead would prove the accuracy of Dragging Canoe's prediction. But if this indomitable warrior who fought so fiercely to hold his wilderness homeland believed that threat of blood or death could restrain the tides of white people who foresaw for the first time a chance to own acres of their own, he did not fathom the nature of those he resisted.

Their names were Henderson and Robertson and Donelson and Sevier and a hundred other plain English and Huguenot and Scottish lines. They wanted all of the essentials and some of the niceties of life. But more than anything else they wanted land, and they wanted to be free. Vigorously, audaciously, relentlessly, they would stake their lives again and again on securing that earth from Indian stewards and that independence from British rulers.

3

Land of the Western Waters

ARLY in September 1780, Col. Isaac Shelby welcomed an unexpected visitor to his home on the Holston River in Virginia. Samuel Philips, a distant Shelby relative and a recent prisoner of the British army, had been paroled by Maj. Patrick Ferguson in order to bring an urgent message to the troublesome men across the mountains. Militia officers on the Watauga, Nolichucky, and Holston rivers were warned that, if they and their followers did not immediately halt any and all opposition to British arms and seek protection under the King's standard, Ferguson would march his army over the mountains, hang their leaders, and lay their country waste with fire and sword. It was just the sort of challenge that would stir these people of the western waters to swift response—of precisely the opposite action demanded.

Isaac Shelby rode at once to Washington County, North Carolina, the area that would soon be northeastern Tennessee, and sought out his old friend, Col. John Sevier. One of the frontiersmen's favorite pastimes, a horse race, with accompanying community barbecue, was in full swing. But Shelby and Sevier separated themselves from the crowd while the sturdy, dignified, somewhat reserved Welsh Virginian told the lithe, frolicsome, immensely popular French Huguenot Tennessean about the British ultimatum. For two days they weighed the situation and made plans.

45

Harried by frontier necessities of daily survival, harassed by sporadic Indian hostilities, the people of these isolated mountain . settlements had had little time or energy to devote to the Revolutionary War ravaging distant battlefields. But Isaac Shelby had some close knowledge of the desperate situation in the South at this moment.

Following the fall of Charleston in the spring of 1780, Shelby, with some six hundred men, had joined Carolina's Col. Charles McDowell and other forces to oppose Lord Cornwallis's northward thrust. During the summer, Shelby had led in minor victories at Thicketty Fort, S.C., and Musgrove's Mill, but any optimism aroused by these successes had been totally routed by the news that on a muggy, hazy sixteenth of August at the important British post of Camden, S.C., the only American army in the Southern colonies had suffered a stunning defeat.

After Camden, Cornwallis—having killed some 900 Americans, taken 1,000 prisoners, captured all the American artillery and most of the wagons and military stores and seen his opposing general, Horatio Gates, flee from the site of disaster "farther and faster than any of his men"—determined to penetrate North Carolina and establish control over that state.

There was, however, one unpredictable factor, one disquieting stronghold that Cornwallis took into consideration. He ordered Maj. Patrick Ferguson, with his Tory militia and Provincial Corps of American Loyalists, into the back country, to arouse support for the king and crush the recalcitrant patriots of northwestern South Carolina, western North Carolina, and the present eastern Tennessee. By this strategy Cornwallis's rear and western flank would be protected. Following these orders, Ferguson had moved northwestward and issued his threatening message on September 7 to the over-mountain men.

Shelby and Sevier now discussed that message. In August, when Shelby had heard of the shattering defeat at Camden, he had turned back toward home and narrowly escaped Ferguson's pursuit. He had some first-hand insight into the low ebb of the American cause throughout the south: food, forage, uniforms, and hope were all in desperately short supply. Every home was a potential battlefield as Patriots and Loyalists killed each other in fierceness of conviction and fear of treachery. Gates's dispirited stragglers could hardly be considered an army. Guerillas, such as the celebrated Swamp Fox, Francis Marion, rode, raided, and disappeared, in lightning strikes that helped keep the Patriot flame flickering throughout the region. A French observer quoted the frequent lament along lowlanders: "Mighty little, mighty few, mighty weak." [1]

In addition, Shelby had to tell Sevier that along with his hateful message, Samuel Philips had brought such information as he could about Ferguson's army. Many were Loyalists who were acquainted with the over-mountain country. One, who had been given a coat of tar and feathers not long before by the men of Capt. Robert Sevier (John's brother), had volunteered to serve as Ferguson's guide along the tortuous mountain routes, should Ferguson decide to invade the frontier.

There is no record of who proposed that the battle should be carried to the enemy, but it was a decision totally characteristic of John Sevier. Contending with Indians, political opponents, or British generals, the fiery frontiersman was not one to sit at home and wait for the issue to be joined. He raided the red men's camps before they could ambush his; he attacked foes before they could marshall their forces against him; why should he wait for the self-confident officer of an oppressive foreign monarch to come and carry out a threat of hanging, fire, and sword?

Whoever proposed the plan, it received enthusiastic response from all the leaders Shelby and Sevier got in touch with after their initial conference. Word raced through the back-country settlements like a leaf-fire before the wind that there would be a general rendezvous for all Patriot volunteers at the Sycamore Shoals.

On the Watauga River, on September 25, where only five years previously the Cherokees had signed their Great Grant to

1. Lucien Agniel, *The American Revolution in the South, 1780–1781* (Riverside, Conn.: Chatham Press, Inc., 1972), p. 70.

the Transylvania Company and to various individual settlers, where the disgruntled Dragging Canoe had uttered his dark curse upon the land, there assembled once again a remarkable ingathering of back-country people.

The scene may well represent one of the definitive moments in Tennessee's history. A thousand men, afoot or on horseback, had come, under various leaders—William Campbell, Shelby, and Sevier—while there was promise of others who would join them along the way. Wives and children had accompanied some of the men to help launch them on their daring expedition. Surrounded by distant mountain ranges, where flaming leaves of sourwood and dogwood foretold the rich Persian carpet of colors yet to come, near the cold, rushing waters of the river fed by a hundred hill-born rivulets, they assembled. Under no force but individual instinct, under no pressure but individual conscience, they collected in common cause.

Appearances were not impressive. Most of the men wore wide-brimmed hats covering their long hair tied in a queue, practical hunting shirts of buckskin, and breeches and gaiters of tan, home-dyed cloth. There were no well-tailored uniforms. There was little visible discipline. Men, women, children, horses, beef cattle for food along the march—all milled about in confusion and excitement. No one was encumbered with baggage: a blanket, a cup, a knapsack of parched corn meal, occasionally a skillet—and the ever-present Deckard, or long rifle. These were their resources.

The atmosphere of that autumn day at Sycamore Shoals was charged with subdued anger awaiting an outlet, secret apprehension awaiting a test, and a vehement ardor that revealed itself in small incidents. One would become a part of Tennessee legend: when James Sevier, not yet sixteen years old, one of John Sevier's ten children by his first wife, yearned to go with his father to meet the British foe but was rejected because he had no horse, the boy's stepmother, young Bonny Kate, interceded for him.

"Here, Mr. Sevier," she said to her husband, "is another of your boys who wants to go with his father and brother Joseph to the war; but we have no horse for him, and, poor fellow, it is too great a distance for him to walk.'' [2] Young James went on the expedition—mounted.

As they prepared to move out on the morning of September 26, their neighbor, the Reverend Samuel Doak, hardy pioneer who had preached his version of the word of God and sowed the seed of education along the western waters, thundered a challenge and a prayer to them and to heaven, concluding with the biblical exhortation, "The sword of the Lord and of Gideon!"

They took up the cry to the Lord. Then they took up their rifles.

Riding or walking, leading or following or herding the cattle, they turned their faces east, unsure of their ultimate destination, certain only of their enemy and their purpose. And who was the hated Ferguson they went to meet? He was a man and a soldier akin in many ways to themselves. A Scottish Highlander, he had begun a brilliant career in the British army at the age of fourteen, serving in the Seven Years War and the West Indies before coming to America. Slender, of medium height, serious, intelligent, he was famous for his courage and coolness under fire and for his skill as a marksman. His unique achievement, however, had been invention of the first breechloading rifle used in the British army—accurate, rapid-firing, dependable even in wet weather.

During the Battle of the Brandywine in 1777, he had received what must have been a crushing blow for a man who reveled in marksmanship: a wound shattered his right elbow and permanently crippled his right arm. Sent south by Sir Henry Clinton to serve at the head of the Loyalist militia, Ferguson did not win Cornwallis's liking or support. He was nonetheless determined to win for himself fame and glory on the battlefield. When Ferguson finally took his stand and decided to engage the Patriots, Cornwallis was only thirty-five miles away in Charlotte, where he had come from Camden. But Ferguson did not heed Cornwallis's messages to avoid a fight. And Cornwallis did not

2. Ramsey, *Annals of Tennessee,* p. 226.

heed Ferguson's need for re-enforcements. The result would prove disastrous for both.

To meet this professional soldier, this acclaimed marksman, the men at Sycamore Shoals set forth on their hard ten-days' march. At first their route crossed rugged mountains along old Indian trails. When they found a blacksmith along the way, they paused and had some of their horses shod. They lost time and patience driving the cattle, especially after a small stampede, and so they butchered all they considered essential for a temporary supply of meat. Then they hurried on through a gap between great old Roan and Yellow mountains. They found snow shoe-mouth deep on the steep slopes; they noted the grassy balds that would puzzle generations of settlers and scientists yet to come. When two of Sevier's men fled in the night, there was a suspicion that the deserters might be going to inform Ferguson of the march and its course. The little army altered its route. They crossed the Blue Ridge, spectacular with autumn's golds and scarlet, and descended into the flatlands, camping beside springs or creeks, near the cabin of a sturdy Irishman or on the farm of a wealthy Tory.

Along the way, like scattered streams feeding into a single river, other "rebels" and their leaders merged with the overmountain boys. When, at last, on the night of October 6, all of the volunteers were gathered together at the Cowpens—site of an extensive cattle enclosure in South Carolina—there were some 1,790 men.

They had elected William Campbell to be their leader. This six-foot-six Virginian, brother-in-law to Patrick Henry, with sturdy, reserved Shelby and the agile, resourceful Sevier, were the central figures without whom there would have been no expedition. In addition, there were such officers as Joseph McDowell, from his Piedmont plantation; corpulent Benjamin Cleveland, with his Wilkes County men; German-born Frederick Hambright from the Catawba River country; South Carolinian James Williams, destined to be the only American colonel killed in this engagement; and Joseph Winston, a leather-tough Virginia frontiersman. Actually, their rank was of minor importance. In the engagement that was to take place on the following day, every man was to follow Shelby's advice: "When we encounter the enemy, don't wait for the word of command. Let each one of you be your own officer." [3]

About nine o'clock on the night of October 6, the "backwater plunderers," as Ferguson had called them, began their final impatient push to find and fight the Tories who had taken their stand at a place called Kings Mountain, just across the South Carolina line. Rain slowed their pace and made heavy going for men and horses alike. After daylight, they came to a cornfield by the roadside, and the men soon stripped the stalks of their heavy ears, feeding their weary horses and shelling raw corn from the cob for their own breakfast. When the rain became a downpour during the morning, the men had to forgo their own comfort to protect their precious rifles. Bags, blankets, and their hunting shirts were wrapped around the flintlocks to keep them dry.

About noon, prospects seemed to brighten. Two Tories were captured and enlisted to pilot the Patriot army the last eight miles to Ferguson's camp, and the rain stopped. A cool breeze ushered in a clear afternoon. They approached Kings Mountain.

To those western frontiersmen who had come from the country of the lofty Roan and the massive Big Blacks (eventually one of these would be named Mt. Mitchell, confirmed as the highest peak east of the Mississippi), the sixteen-mile-long Kings Mountain range with several pinnacles would have seemed familiar enough, but the Kings Mountain ridge where the Tories had taken their stand must have appeared as little more than a potato-hill in their gardens back home. Slanting some 600 yards in a northeasterly direction, it rose only 60 feet above the surrounding countryside and ranged in width from 60 to 120 feet. Springs providing plentiful water had offered an advantage for Ferguson. Timber that reached almost to ridge summit and then thinned out along the crest would prove a decisive disadvantage for Ferguson. In traditional warfare, defense of such a position would have seemed advantageous. But this was

3. Samuel Cole Williams, *Tennessee During the Revolutionary War* (1944; reprint edition, Knoxville: University of Tennessee Press, 1974), p. 151.

frontier warfare; and back-country men would not wage it in proper European military fashion, but in Indian style.

About a mile from the ridge, the Patriots hitched their horses, divided into four columns, and quietly moved to surround the ridge in positions that had been assigned each leader. Experienced squirrel hunters from the hills must have appreciated at that moment the damp, soaked leaves that cushioned their footfalls as they moved to surprise Patrick Ferguson. They succeeded, and the ridge was almost surrounded before British pickets discovered their presence.

The Patriots charged the hill with their flintlocks blazing and their shouts echoing through the hills. A participant later recalled, "The mountain appeared volcanic; there flashed along its summit and around its base, and up its sides, one long sulphurous blaze." [4] Meeting Tory fire and bayonets, the Patriots fell back down the slopes. But in the ravine they paused, reloaded, reformed, and using trees and boulders as cover, they stormed the ridge once more. The enemy, drawn up in close-column formation along the ridge's crest, presented a fair mark for the mountain men's aim.

The crux of the battle was summed up in the later judgment that Kings Mountain proved "more assailable by the rifle than defensible with the bayonet." When the Tories did attempt volley-firing at their assailants, their elevation caused them to overshoot and leave most of their targets untouched. Meanwhile, the deadly aim of the farmer-hunters and Indian fighters was reaping a heavy toll. Ferguson, wearing a checkered shirt over his uniform and blowing a silver whistle, galloped from one threatened part of his precarious position to another, rallying his men, defying danger. But the advancing cries of the Patriots were not to be quelled.

"Here they are, my brave boys. Shout like hell and fight like devils." [5] Thus Campbell launched his attack.

4. George C. Mackenzie, *Kings Mountain*, National Park Service Historical Handbook Series, No. 22 (Washington, D.C.: Government Printing Office, 1955), p. 20.

5. Lyman C. Draper, *King's Mountain and Its Heroes: History of the Battle of King's Mountain and the Events Which Led to It* (1881; reprint edition, Baltimore: Genealogical Publishing Co., 1971), p. 247.

"Look out for Ferguson with his sword in his left hand, wearing a light hunting-shirt." [6] The watchword was passed from soldier to soldier.

"Boys, quickly re-load your rifles, let's advance upon them and give them another hell of a fire." [7] It was Shelby urging his men on in the midst of the fight.

"Let us at it again!" a man from the Holston country called.[8]

The very mountain seemed to thunder.

"Face to the hill!" [9] A major had just shouted the command when a British ball struck him, and he fell.

Several Negro servants had accompanied the Patriot colonels on this expedition. Those who took up arms now acquitted themselves well in the battle.

The surge, the shouts, the confusion intensified. The defenders along the ridge-top were squeezed into the rapidly shrinking space of the command post along the broadest northeast portion of the crest. The Tories became ever more exposed targets. A few white handkerchiefs appeared, but Ferguson cut them down. His silver whistle blew shrilly above the melee, his bayonet and rallying cries seemed to be everywhere. "Huzza, brave boys! The day is our own." [10] His cries of encouragement were punctuated by blasts of the whistle.

Suddenly, surrounded by a few officers, Ferguson spurred his horse. Slashing with his sword he plunged in a headlong dash through the advancing line and down the steep slope. In a hail of fire, he fell from the saddle.

A man in Sevier's command named Robert Young believed that his rifle, "Sweet-Lips," had claimed the life of the British leader. But there were seven other bullets in Ferguson's body; both arms were broken, his hat and clothing were shredded to rags.

Captain Abraham de Peyster, Tory second-in-command, took Ferguson's place. From the outset, de Peyster had not thought

6. Draper, *King's Mountain*, p. 275.
7. Draper, *King's Mountain*, p. 252.
8. Draper, *King's Mountain*, p. 251.
9. Draper, *King's Mountain*, p. 257.
10. Draper, *King's Mountain*, p. 273.

either the site or the engagement wise, and now he lost no time in attempting to surrender. But he discovered that it was easier to begin than to end a fight with the over-mountain men. Many of the Americans did not seem to understand about a white flag, and the few that did chose not to comprehend its meaning, so that, even after submission, the slaughter continued.

"Cease firing! For God's sake, cease firing!" [11] Colonel Campbell was forced to gallop along the line and quell the rampant energy and rage he had helped unleash so short a time before.

De Peyster, sitting on his grey horse, uttered the laconic remonstrance to Campbell about the firing on his flag of truce that it was unfair.

Memory of the hated British Colonel Banastre Tarleton, who had refused quarter to vanquished Whigs in recent battles, spurred many of the backcountry men to continue firing.

When, at last, the killing ceased, three "huzzas for Liberty" resounded across Kings Mountain ridge. Scattered along its crest and slopes were 28 dead and 64 wounded Americans; 1,018 British casualties, and 698 to be marched off as prisoners.

The body of Patrick Ferguson—minus the silver whistle, carried off as a trophy by one of the victors—was buried in a small cup-shaped hollow on the slope where he died. Buried with him was the camp-follower remembered only as Virginia Sal. Rocks were piled cairn-like atop the grave to discourage wolves from disturbing the burial site. "We are kings of Kings Mountain," he had said, "and all the rebels in hell cannot drive me from it." [12] At age thirty-six, Highlander Patrick Ferguson, whose mother had worried and yearned over his early days in the army at age fourteen, whose accuracy as a marksman had been erased by a shattered elbow, who had recklessly defied America's highlanders, was not driven from the mountain—he was left there forever.

Ferguson was the only non-American on either side engaged in this battle. Kings Mountain was a struggle between "broth-

11. Draper, *King's Mountain*, p. 283.
12. Draper, *King's Mountain*, p. 211.

ers,'' the bitter kind of hostility Tennesseans would experience during various crises in their history, as deeply held ideologies and allegiances clashed in brutal conflict.

The acrimony inherent in such conflict surfaced during the days following Kings Mountain. On their homeward journey, the victorious Patriots held an impromptu court for thirty of the most hated prisoners. Conditions were not ripe for mercy. Victors and vanquished, eager to reach their destination, found it slow going as they were encumbered with the large number of wounded and few conveyances. Food was so scarce that green pumpkins discovered in a field along the roadside were gathered and fried and seemed to the hungry men to be the sweetest eating imaginable. Corn on the ear and raw pumpkin were thrown to the prisoners, who scrambled to gnaw on it. Starving, impatient, remembering friends or relatives left behind on the field of battle, informed daily of Tory raids against the homes of Patriots throughout the countryside, the Patriots' appetite for revenge was whetted, sharpened. They felt the need to make an example. And so they convicted thirty of the prisoners who were chosen to stand impromptu trial. A dozen were forthwith condemned to hanging. By the light of pine-knot torches, on a gaunt old tree known thereafter as the Gallows Oak, nine men were hanged, three at a time. The last three were reprieved. They joined their fellow prisoners to be taken, under Cleveland's command, to Hillsboro, North Carolina.

The strange, spontaneous little army disbanded and returned to the many sources from which it had gathered. Over-mountain men hastened to their homes along the Nolichucky, the Watauga, and the Holston rivers. They had gone out to meet a threat head-on. Like Bre'r Rabbit in the briar patch, they found that the foxiness of Ferguson had thrown them into a terrain and situation exactly suited to their capabilities. They were mountain men, fighting on a mountain. They were woodsmen, engaging in a wooded area. They were unregimented individualists, meeting in man-to-man combat. Their long rifles provided a range (100 to 200 yards) that let them stay clear of the fire of British muskets (30 to 40 yards' range), while they crouched behind trees or boulders to reload and take careful aim once more, diminishing the importance of the superior British firepower and speed in loading. The trees around them prevented the organized bayonet charge in which Ferguson could have excelled. And their spirit, as well as their surroundings, was adapted to the personal, Indian-style assault that recognized only the most essential command while accepting the fullest individual responsibility for victory and valor sometimes bordering on recklessness.

News of Kings Mountain chilled Cornwallis as he waited in Charlotte. If Commander-in-Chief Sir Henry Clinton, at his headquarters in New York, was inclined to dismiss lightly the loss of Ferguson and his relatively small force at some improbable little mountain in the Southern hinterlands, he would eventually come to a different evaluation of that event. Clinton would one day speak of Kings Mountain as "the first link in a chain of evils that followed each other in regular succession until they at last ended in the total loss of America." [13]

The spirits of patriots everywhere were revived by the victory at Kings Mountain. Tories and the British invaders were not invincible. Those loyal to the Crown grew more hesitant in their support. Guerilla warfare expanded across the Carolinas. A new American general assumed command in the South and used the newly revived hopes to fuel a fresh military initiative.

The march from Kings Mountain to Yorktown would take a year. In the September shortly before Kings Mountain, General George Washington was writing Count de Rochambeau that the Patriots' cause was tottering. In October of the following year, Washington was receiving Cornwallis's surrender at Yorktown. The little Patriot army at Kings Mountain had played a part in rescuing its country from the brink of defeat.

Writing four decades later, Thomas Jefferson said, "I remember well the deep and grateful impression made on the mind of every one by that memorable victory. It was the joyful annunciation of that turn of the tide of success which terminated

13. Mark M. Boatner, III, *Encyclopedia of the American Revolution* (New York: David Mackay Co., 1966), p. 582.

the Revolutionary War with the seal of our independence.'' [14]

Not all, or even a majority, of the army had been over-mountain men in that "memorable victory.'' There had been a dozen colonels and many lesser officers leading the forces. Yet, the Tennesseans, as they would soon be called, and their leader, John Sevier, became the symbol and image that would persist through two centuries of recollection—and also neglect—of this brief, bloody, consequential encounter.

And there were at least three elements that emerged at Kings Mountain that would become part of both the legend and the reality of a later and more tragic conflict awaiting all Tennesseans.

The first was the Indian war-whoop adopted by the hill men at Kings Mountain. It aroused special attention and comment by numerous participants in the battle. Captain de Peyster spoke of its perpetrators as "the damned yelling boys.'' Later historians were to wonder if this was the parent of the rebel yell that would play such a psychological role in Civil War battles.

Second, the term *outliers,* in use at the time of the Revolution, meant, to Ferguson and others who spoke it, those patriots who left their families at home and hid out, either to avoid taking an oath of allegiance to the king or to escape the vengeance of neighbors on the opposite side. The word indicated the grim personal nature of this civil conflict. It would assume even sharper meaning during the following century's conflict when *outliers* became a word and an experience in many homes.

Finally, Kings Mountain revealed the resources of leadership that existed in the back country. One historian would comment on the "considerable number of outstanding leaders, and the remarkable thing is how successfully they worked together.'' [15] American historian George Bancroft said: "It is not to be imagined that the assemblage of the troops was an accidental and tumultuous congregation of men, merely seeking wild adventures. On the contrary, although each step in the progress of the enterprise seemed to be characterized by a daring impulse,

14. Draper, *King's Mountain,* p. 585.
15. Boatner, *Encyclopedia of the Revolution,* p. 582.

yet the purpose had been coolly conceived and its execution de-
liberately planned in a temper of no less wisdom than hardi-
hood." [16]

Those leaders who had assembled at Sycamore Shoals and
their later companions knew how to rally men. It was a genius
and an art possessed and practiced by each of those varied, val-
iant, and quite human leaders who were becoming Tennessee's
first heroes. They could rally their neighbors, not only for
battle, but for more sustained and enduring struggles as well.

16. Draper, *King's Mountain*, p. 375.

4

Settlement and
Self-Government

WHILE some of the settlers on the western waters returned east of the mountains to thwart a British expedition into the border country, others were turning toward the west to meet the challenge there. It was the continuing familiar challenge—land—breeding a new, particularly American kind of leader. His name would be Boone and Crockett, Henderson and Blount, Robertson and Sevier and Jackson. He would be trailblazer and long hunter, entrepreneur and land speculator, settler and politician, and always, but always, Indian fighter. For the land did not yield easily, simply for the taking.

"The manless land beckoned to the landless man."

There was a flaw in that truism: part of it was not true. The vast forests, hills, and meadows stretching to the interior were "manless" of whites, but they made up extensive hunting and homing grounds that were basic to the red man's way of life. Land that appeared to the white stranger empty of all claim and destiny might be filled with traditions and resources that the native users believed to be indispensable—and theirs by right of spirit, as well as possession. But to each it beckoned.

The white man moved to make that land his in a variety of ways: by conquest and purchase from the Indians; by armed rejection of French, British, or Spanish claims; by blood and sweat during hundreds of brutal encounters along the shifting boundaries, and by superlative effort of will and muscle during long days and decades of settlement as the status of the region shifted from British colony to North Carolina county to territory to sovereign state.

Cunning and strategy were summoned, too. No less an idealist than Thomas Jefferson offered this realistic, perhaps cynical, appraisal of the coveted Chickasaw lands of West Tennessee and Kentucky and the possibility of their acquisition:

> The method by which we may advance towards our object will be, to establish among them a factory or factories for furnishing them with all necessaries and comforts they may wish (spiritous liquors excepted), and encouraging these, and especially their leading men, to run in debt beyond their individual means of paying; and, whenever in that situation, they will always cede lands to rid themselves of debt. A factory about the Chickasaw Bluffs would be tolerably central. . . . This tribe is very poor, and they want necessaries with which we abound. We want lands with which they abound, and these natural wants seem to offer fair ground of mutual supply.[1]

Speculation on a grandiose scale was behind much of the exploration and settlement. Richard Henderson, whose dreams were as expansive as the landscape, was considered by a contemporary to be an extraordinary person, an eccentric genius. A sympathetic historian has called him an activist dreamer with a colonizer's genius and a speculative capitalist's ambition. Henderson was frustrated in his Kentucky ventures with Daniel Boone to establish Transylvania as the fourteenth American colony. Virginia and North Carolina annulled that immense purchase—but granted Henderson's company a consolation of 200,000 acres in the Cumberland River country.

By the time of the engagement at Kings Mountain, there were more than three hundred settlers living in scattered stations along the Cumberland, abiding by a social contract they called the "Cumberland Compact." Although they were still considered part of Washington County, North Carolina, their remote-

---

1. Williams, *Beginnings of West Tennessee*, p. 84.

ness from the seat of county government made some local rules and laws necessary. Thus the agreement had come into being, written by Henderson, probably with the counsel of the two able men who had led initial settlers: James Robertson and John Donelson.

The Cumberland Compact revealed several interesting facts about the competence of these first Middle Tennesseans. There was the question of literacy. Only one out of the 256 settlers who signed that Compact left a mark rather than signature on the document. There was the matter of insight into human nature and foresight into the nature of the government required, as indicated by a provision for the recall of any of the twelve "Triers," or judges, who governed the community of scattered stations, should he prove derelict in his duty. This was a very new, even rare, concept at that time. And finally, signers of the Compact freely assumed responsibility along with rights: "We do not desire to be exempt from the rateable share of the public expense of the present war, or other contingent charges of government." [2]

They had arrived here, on the raw edge of the frontier, during the winter of 1779–1780, waging their own struggle to victory. It was called "the cold winter." Freeze set in early and would not loose its grip. Snowfall came in November. But the two men Henderson had chosen to lead his settlers were undaunted. James Robertson would take a party overland, while John Donelson piloted another group along the water route to the French Lick, later named Nashville.

James Robertson—Scotch-Irish, quiet, steadfast, taught to read and write by his wife after they were married—has been called the father of Tennessee. He merits the honor. In the east, on the Watauga River, in 1771, he established a colony that became the nucleus of the future state. In the west, at the Chickasaw agency, he improved Indian-white relationships during years crucial to the state's survival. And in between, he helped

2. A. W. Putnam, *History of Middle Tennessee: or, Life & Times of General James Robertson,* Tennesseana Editions Series (1859; reprint edition, Knoxville: University of Tennessee Press, 1971), p. 100.

found the state's capital city in Middle Tennessee. It was the force of his personality, as much as any single factor, that carried the journey to the Cumberland and the establishment of Fort Nashborough to eventual success.

Late in that bleak fall of 1779, Robertson's party left the Watauga. After following the Wilderness Road into Kentucky, they turned southwest. Late in December, having been joined by other settlers along the way, they arrived at French Lick. Ice on the river was so solid that cattle and horses could be driven across it to the site that would soon be Fort Nashborough. Their journey had been harsh and demanding, but it cost no lives and suffered no Indian attacks. The same could not be said of the effort that brought the other segment of settlers by water.

On December 22, John Donelson made the first entry in his "Journal of a Voyage, intended by God's permission, in the good boat Adventure, from Fort Patrick Henry, on Holston river to the French Salt Springs on Cumberland river." [3] The wife and five of James Robertson's eleven children, as well as Donelson's wife, Rachel Stockley, and daughter, fifteen-year-old Rachel, who would become Mrs. Andrew Jackson in future years, were among those on the thirty-odd flatboats, dugouts, and canoes that composed the little flotilla. It had been said that "the Donelson fleet has the same relation to the history of the old Southwest that the *Mayflower* has to New England." [4]

On April 24, 1780, Donelson could record in his final entry the long overdue arrival at their destination. During the four months of their journey, the hardy venturers had experienced Indian attacks, an outbreak of smallpox, hunger, fatigue, and bone-chilling cold. Among the thirty-three casualties had been two Negroes, one dead by drowning, the other from frostbite and infection. At a particularly dangerous stretch of the Tennessee River known as the Whirl, or Suck, at the foot of the great promontory of Lookout Mountain, one of the boats wrecked on a large rock while being fired upon by the Chickamauga Indians

    3. Ramsey, *Annals of Tennessee*, p. 197.
    4. Donald Davidson, *The Tennessee: The Old River, Frontier to Secession*, Rivers of America Series (New York: Holt, Rinehart & Winston, 1946), 1:155.

along the shore. Effort to save the boat was joined by all the women, working in the wet and cold. One woman had only the night before given birth to a child. The baby was killed in the haste and confusion; the woman's name was recorded only as Mrs. Peyton. When the boat was finally dislodged, Mrs. Peyton's dress, like that of Mrs. Jennings and of the Negro woman helping them, hung on her weary body wet, limp, cold, and shredded by bullets.

Perhaps the low point of the entire voyage came for John Donelson on March 15, when the party arrived at the mouth of the Tennessee River, where it joined the Ohio. Donelson recorded the moment in his journal:

> The river is very high, and the current rapid, our boats not constructed for the purpose of stemming a rapid stream, our provision exhausted, the crews almost worn down with hunger and fatigue, and know not what distance we have to go, or what time it will take us to our place of destination. The scene is rendered still more melancholy, as several boats will not attempt to ascend the rapid current. Some intend to descend the Mississippi to Natchez; others are bound for the Illinois—among the rest my son-in-law and daughter. We now part, perhaps to meet no more, for I am determined to pursue my course, happen what will.[5]

His determination won its goal. At the end of a thousand tortuous miles, they found a cedar-dotted bluff above an icy river. The prospects at the little settlement were dreary. But they forged their compact of government, drew on corn brought from Boonesborough, Kentucky, to sustain them till they could raise a crop the following year, and they prevailed.

It was a precarious existence. The Cumberland settlements often seemed on the brink of annihilation. Robertson and his stoical settlers withstood both disorganized raids and well-planned attacks by Creek warriors and the fierce Chickamaugans under Dragging Canoe, who had vowed to fight for every parcel of the red man's land. Robertson negotiated peace with the more amenable Chickasaws. He watched his settlement grow. Following the Revolution, North Carolina rewarded soldiers

5. Ramsey, *Annals of Tennessee,* p. 201.

who had fought for the American cause by setting aside a large portion of upper Middle Tennessee to provide land bounties, ranging from 640 acres for a private to 12,000 acres for a brigadier general. When Davidson County was formed, Robertson was chosen to represent it in the North Carolina legislature. When the Tennessee Country became the Territory of the United States South of the River Ohio, General Robertson was made commander of the militia. As U.S. agent to the Chickasaws, he fulfilled his final public office, dying near Memphis in 1814. His Nashborough, grown to Nashville, had survived and flourished.

Survival was more than the brief and dramatic State of Franklin achieved. What it could claim was one of the most charismatic leaders who ever galloped through Tennessee history. And John Sevier galloped more often than he walked: from Rockingham County, Virginia, where he was born in 1745, to the Watauga settlement in 1772; from Watauga to Kings Mountain; along the lonely little line of cabins and forts threatened by Indian attack during his twenty years as acknowledged leader of every important Indian campaign along the Tennessee border. His fame was summarized in a statistic: of thirty-five battles fought, he had won thirty-five victories.

The men who rode with him called him "Chucky Jack," after the Nolichucky River farm which was his home, and they gave him complete and unswerving loyalty. The state of North Carolina could arrest him for being governor in the rebellious separatist movement of Franklin, and his friends would snatch him from the very courtroom and leave the legalisms to perish by default. The U.S. government could suspect him of conversing with the Spanish in an effort to secure attention and support for neglected Western lands and needs, and his followers would disregard any charge of conspiracy and cut the rumor to wither at its source. They liked his style.

His quarrels were explosive, in the best frontier tradition: with John Tipton, who remained loyal to North Carolina during the Franklin statehood, Sevier engaged in a pitched battle at the latter's farm; with Andrew Jackson, a political rival, he indulged in challenges to duel—which were never realized—and street encounters involving brandished canes and drawn pistols. His family life was exemplary by frontier standards: two wives (of whom, one—Bonny Kate—jumped a stockade into his arms while fleeing Indian pursuers) and eighteen children.

Perhaps Sevier's unique characteristic on the western scene was his ability to unite in his own personality the refinements of an educated gentleman with the ruggedness of a pragmatic frontiersman. Descendant of a well-born French Huguenot family, originally named Xavier, he was spirited, tactful, handsome. Slightly under six feet tall, lithe and graceful, with light brown hair and a Roman profile boasting strong nose and chin, John Sevier seems the epitome of much that has come to characterize our image of the early Tennessean—indeed, the early American. One historian has described him as an individualist in every sense. "There is no other character like him in border annals. He was cavalier and prince in his leadership of men; he had their homage. Yet he knew how to be comrade and brother to the lowliest. He won and held the confidence and friendship of the serious-minded Robertson no less than the idolatry of the wildest spirits on the frontier . . . he could outride and outshoot—and, it is said, outswear—the best and the worst of the men who followed him." [6] Another chronicler closer to his time has confirmed Sevier's appeal: "He was fluent, colloquial, and gallant—frolicsome, generous and convivial—well informed rather than well read. Of books he knew little. Men, he had studied well and accurately." [7]

These men followed him to Kings Mountain, on retaliatory raids against Indian villages, and into the venture of a new state—although in the latter enterprise there was some ambiguity as to whether Sevier led or followed the impulses of a citizenry angered and frustrated by the remoteness and indifference of its parent state.

Frankland, Land of the Free: easily romanticized by local writers and ignored by national historians. Its drama deserved

6. Constance Lindsey Skinner, *Pioneers of the Old Southwest* (New Haven: Yale University Press, 1919), p. 169.

7. Ramsey, *Annals of Tennessee*, p. 108.

neither distortion nor neglect. As symptom of a conflict between federal bureaucracy and local autonomy, it reveals, early on, an ailment that would persist long after the little state had disappeared. As an example of common public needs and desires shaped and used by powerful private interests allied with international ambitions, the aborted frontier state was forerunner of numerous similar chapters in American history. Perhaps its mixture of idealism and shrewdness was best illustrated when Sevier, while writing a letter to Benjamin Franklin, impulsively altered the name from *Frankland* to *Franklin,* in the hope that the subtle flattery would win support of the great statesman for this struggling state.

In reality, money was a deep though often obscured motive behind the movement for the new state. One Tennessee history has summarized this part of the situation:

> Important in the background of the Franklin movement was the "Land Grab Act" of 1783 pushed through the North Carolina legislature by William Blount and other land speculators. This law offered for sale at a price of ten pounds (about five dollars in view of the depreciation of the currency) per hundred acres all unappropriated land in the Tennessee country, which was soon to be ceded to the United States, with the exception of military counties and a Cherokee Reservation east of the Tennessee River and south of the French Broad and Big Pigeon. Although the land office remained open only seven months, nearly four million acres of land were entered, thus creating the foundations for large fortunes of several future Tennesseans.[8]

On August 24, 1784, and in November and December, delegates from Washington, Sullivan, and Greene counties met, first at Jonesborough, then Greeneville, and again at Jonesborough, as they seceded from North Carolina to form an independent state. Their reasons were clearly stated and involved two basic factors. The first was geography. Distance from the seat of government and the intervening mountains made North Carolina ignorant of the back country's needs and indifferent to its dangers. Franklinites doubtless agreed with the statement that "Kings

8. Folmsbee, Corlew, and Mitchell, *Tennessee,* p. 79.

Mountain forever settled the fact that the Watauga people were much better able to protect and assist North Carolina than North Carolina was to assist and protect the Watauga people.'' [9]

A second factor was the ambiguous position in which the territory found itself—ceded by North Carolina to the federal government, which had not yet accepted it. There was the feeling that the people living there must form their own government or endure anarchy.

William Cocke's motion at Jonesborough/Jonesboro for a new state, and the subsequent declaration of independence and adoption of a constitution by Frankland/Franklin, appear to be the last clear-cut features of the enterprise. Confusion and conflict prevailed during its four years of existence.

North Carolina, having discovered that the federal government would not repay it for certain Indian expeditions involving these western lands if they were surrendered to the U.S., repealed its act of cession. But the Westerners were already launched on their course. Unable to reconcile differences between the old state of North Carolina and the new Franklin, Sevier accepted the latter's governorship in March 1785.

Now there were two governments. With which were the Cherokees to make agreements and sign treaties? Which should have jurisdiction over the courts? What currency would be used? These were a few of the practicalities to be resolved. At least one of them, involving money, was met with dispatch. Franklin provided for officials' salaries to be paid at the rate of one thousand deerskins for the governor, five hundred for the state treasurer, four hundred and fifty otter skins for the governor's secretary, five hundred raccoon skins for each county clerk, and for a constable serving a warrant—one mink skin.

Division on more serious questions cut deep, however. Personal animosity between Governor Sevier and North Carolina loyalist John Tipton erupted in open combat before it settled into a bitter, lifelong feud. Adherents of the ''Old State'' contested the ''Franklinites'' in the courtroom, at the voting booth,

9. Samuel Gordon Heiskell, *Andrew Jackson and Early Tennessee History,* 3 vols. (Nashville: Ambrose, 1918, 1920–1921), 1:40–41.

and over the Treaty of Dumplin Creek, by which the Cherokees released another large segment of land for settlement. It was the white people living on this land south of the French Broad River who remained most fiercely partisan to the State of Franklin—with good reason. Most of them had pushed onto these acres illegally. North Carolina had designated them Indian territory. But many a land-hungry settler, eying the rich river-bottoms and the wooded coves and hills of this "unused" country had staked his future and would risk his life to remain here. In the bloody skirmishes between Cherokees and Franklinites, war reaped its usual harvest of innocent victims and horrors. The tragedy of Old Tassel and the Kirks was all too typical of episodes past and yet to come in America's history.

In the spring of 1788, the family of John Kirk lived on the Little River, a dozen miles south of the present city of Knoxville. One morning the Kirk home was visited by Slim Tom, a Cherokee the Kirks had befriended on many previous occasions. While they gave him food, Slim Tom noted that Kirk and his son, John, Jr., were absent. Slim Tom left, but soon returned with a band of warriors. When the two Kirk men came home a little later, they found the eleven members of their family dead and scalped.

News of the massacre inflamed the frontier. Officials were hesitant to retaliate, however, without specific orders from North Carolina. But Sevier's term as governor of the floundering State of Franklin had just expired—and he was never one to refuse an Indian raid. Once more he would prove to his neighbors that, in time of stress, they could turn to him. With 150 men, including an avid Indian hater, James Hubbard, and John Kirk, Jr., Sevier rode against the Cherokee villages. He was met by two revered peace chiefs, Old Tassel and Abram, and he received their pledges of friendship. Then the party rode on to the town of Hiwassee and burned it. Afterward, Sevier and Hubbard separated; the latter was to go to Chilhowee and destroy that town, where Slim Tom lived.

On his way to Chilhowee, Hubbard invited Old Tassel to accompany him to a talk with Abram. When they arrived, the two old chiefs met with two other well-known leaders under a flag of truce Hubbard had raised. As soon as they had gathered, Hubbard closed the door, posted guards at the windows, handed a tomahawk to John Kirk, Jr., and invited him to take vengeance for his dead loved ones.

It was a bloody business. Old Tassel, unarmed and resigned, bowed his head and received the death blow. The others followed his example. Even the pioneers, who often found it difficult to like any Indian, had respected Old Tassel. They found him to be a statesman of integrity and an orator who spoke truth.

This was a low point of Southern frontier history. Sevier, not directly involved, was nevertheless held in part responsible—he was the leader, and he had put Hubbard and Kirk in charge of a potentially violent situation. There was fear that warfare would now become even more intense. The governor of North Carolina charged Sevier with treason and issued a warrant for his arrest. John Tipton took Sevier into custody and transported him across the mountains to a North Carolina jail. But Chucky Jack was not without supporters. In Morganton, General Charles McDowell, Sevier's old companion from Kings Mountain, provided him bail. And when a group of family and friends came from across the mountains, they rescued Sevier and he simply rode home with them. Charges against him lapsed, as the State of Franklin faded out of existence.

One other force was exerting at this time a strange and powerful pressure on John Sevier, James Robertson, and the area that would soon become Tennessee. This influence was the continuing Spanish presence along the Gulf of Mexico and west of the Mississippi.

British defeat in the Revolution had left Spain fearful for what could happen to its colonial possessions in America. There were moves to bind Indian allegiance to Spain ever more closely, intrigues to promote western dissatisfaction with the Atlantic seaboard, and threats of limiting navigation on the Mississippi. To achieve any or all of these maneuvers, Don Estevan Miro, who became Governor of Louisiana in 1785, wielded an artful and persuasive pen toward James Robertson on the Cumberland and Sevier, "His Excellency of Franklin."

Robertson was sufficiently friendly with the Spanish governor to persuade North Carolina to name the Cumberland region the "Mero District." Sevier entered into long and complicated discussion with the Spanish leaders. Plot? Intrigue? Sophisticated maneuver for balance of power? By whatever name they are labeled, the unorthodox negotiations eventually came to naught.

Franklin returned to its original status as Washington, Sullivan, and Greene counties, and then, through a second cession by North Carolina, enlarged to include the Cumberland settlements, it became the Territory of the United States South of the River Ohio, from 1790 to 1796. William Blount was territorial governor. And if Robertson was the father of Tennessee and Sevier its spirit, Blount might be cast as its entrepreneur, its early-day "developer." He and his brothers enjoyed a sizable interest in this country: more than a million acres of western land. If Blount's immense private investments threatened a conflict of interest with the public's welfare, no one posed the question. At "Rocky Mount," in the forks of the Holston and Watauga rivers, he established the capitol of the Southwest Territory, then removed it to White's Fort, which he renamed Knoxville, in honor of the U.S. Secretary of War, Henry Knox, whose aid for the western frontiers was of paramount importance. The two-story frame house built by Blount was the first west of the Alleghenies and was considered a mansion. When the Territorial legislature established Blount College (eventually the University of Tennessee) in 1794, his daughter, Barbara Gray Blount, became one of the first co-eds in America.

Blount recognized Sevier's influence. In accounting for one concession made to the General, he explained that Sevier's name carried more terror to the Cherokees than would a regiment of ordinary men. Throughout the region's shift in status, the popular confidence in Sevier was evident in his selection, first, as senator in the North Carolina General Assembly and then his election to the United States Congress—he was the first member of that body from the Mississippi valley—and, finally, appointment by President George Washington as brigadier-general of the territorial forces. When Americans received full right to navigation of the Mississippi, in 1795, Spanish intrigue, which had been part of white and red conflict in the Tennessee country for so long, came to an end.

John Sevier's public career was only beginning. Tennessee was admitted into the Union the following year, 1796, and Sevier became the state's first governor. Six times he was elected governor; four times he was elected a Representative to the U.S. Congress. At the close of his last term, in 1815, he went on a boundary commission to the Creek country and there, in a tent, on the frontier he knew so intimately and represented so completely, Chucky Jack died of fever.

James Robertson had died only the year before, among the Chickasaws. It was peculiarly appropriate that each of these hardy, venturesome men who had spent so much time and energy in Indian confrontations should come to the end of his life among the strangers who were also brothers in their love of this land and its freedom. Different as these two early Tennesseans were, they represented something different from the Hendersons and the Blounts and many soon to follow. They "preferred to serve, survey, and save the people, than to blaze and block, chip and chop, lot and plot, the richest lands." [10]

Towering above all of these, however, was the irascible, generous, brilliant personality and lean, hawklike countenance of the leader who would blast the western winds of change across the country and into Washington itself. Andrew Jackson, like John Sevier, was a loyal lover and a fierce hater; a man who invited strong devotion or dislike, but never neutrality. (It has been said of Jackson's hatred of his fellow westerner, Henry Clay, that it became an archetype, a sort of landmark, a means of measuring other hatreds for generations.) Probably no two of its leaders ever captured more of the spirit or adulation of Tennessee than Sevier and Jackson. When Sevier was elected the state's first governor, Jackson was chosen to be its first Representative in Washington. But for each other, these men enjoyed only the most bitter enmity.

Cause for that enmity was rooted in early political differences

---

10. Putnam, *History of Middle Tennessee,* p. 63.

and these were strained beyond all reconciliation when the two quarreled on the streets of Knoxville one day: as Jackson referred to his service for his country, Sevier supposedly replied, "Services? I know of no great service you have rendered the country except taking a trip to Natchez with another man's wife." [11]

If these two hot-headed men had been armed that day with anything more than Jackson's sword cane and Sevier's cutlass, the course of American history would doubtless have been altered. Sevier had salted the one wound that never healed for Andrew Jackson: the disgrace and scorn and, maybe worst of all, the polite snickers and whispers directed against his beloved Rachel because of an unfortunate misunderstanding at the time of their marriage.

Rachel Donelson, lively, dark-haired, courageous daughter of John Donelson, had married Lewis Robards, of Kentucky. The marriage was not a happy one, and they separated. When Jackson read in a newspaper that Robards had been granted a divorce by the Virginia legislature, he proposed to the attractive girl he had known since he was a young lawyer newly arrived in Nashville from Piedmont Carolina. Rachel and Andrew were married in Natchez, where she had fled to escape Robards's threats. Two years later, they discovered that Robards had only applied for, not received, a divorce. Rachel had been living in bigamy. Now the divorce was accomplished, the wedding re-enacted. But material had been provided to fuel opposition rumor and innuendo in political campaigns for years to come. And Jackson was ready for them: for thirty-three long years, he kept his pistols polished and in condition for instant use against anyone who cast a shadow of discredit or doubt on the honor of the woman he loved with such single-minded and fierce and gentle devotion that it made him at once a paradox and a paragon to both friends and enemies.

Of enemies, Andrew Jackson had wide choice and experience. There were the universal enemies—death, disease, and

---

11. Marquis James, *The Life of Andrew Jackson* (Indianapolis: Bobbs-Merrill, 1933), p. 92.

war—that he met while still a boy. His father died before he was born on the Carolina border, March 15, 1767. By the time he was fifteen, tall, gangling, almost red-headed, Andy had been a bushwhacker for the American Revolutionary patriots, and a prisoner. His refusal to polish British boots had won him a giant scar across his head when an officer laid open the boy's scalp with his sword. His two older brothers died in the war, one of the smallpox that almost claimed Andy's life. When his mother died of fever contracted while she was nursing patriot prisoners in Charleston, he was left without a family. The ancient adversaries seemed to have won. But as with a procession of political, military, and personal enemies yet to come, they had reckoned without the spirit of the proud, shy, dangerous young frontiersman. The scar across his head was as nothing compared to the scar on his memory. "At fifteen," one biographer says, "he did not know soldiering, but he knew war." [12] And wars were for keeps. Life and death. Wars were to win. Andy Jackson usually won.

As a young lawyer who came from Salisbury, North Carolina, to set up office in Nashville in 1788, "he knew the art of persuading juries that his was the cause of justice, and with that art at his command he could win verdicts in frontier courts over any opponent who seemed to have the law, but not justice, on his side." [13]

Elected to the House of Representatives in 1796, to the Senate in 1798, and in service six years as a justice on the state Supreme Court, Jackson sought office, resigned, engaged in duels, accumulated land, and faced financial ruin in the panic of 1798, which left him with a deep-seated western suspicion of banks. He was made a major-general in the militia.

Then another war came, and Jackson's talent for winning made him a hero. With Tennessee volunteers and some friendly Indians, he entered the War of 1812, for which it seemed nobody was really prepared. New England grumbled, and there were

12. Gerald W. Johnson, *Andrew Jackson* (New York: Minton, Balch & Co., 1927), p. 34.

13. G. W. Johnson, *Andrew Jackson,* p. 53.

hints of secession. But on March 27, 1814, at the Horseshoe Bend of the Tallapoosa River, in territory that later became Alabama, Jackson won a signal victory over British Indian allies and broke forever the might of the Creek nation. With only forty-nine casualties among his forces, he left 557 opposing warriors dead on the battlefield. By no authority but his own, he marched down to Florida and in November crushed a British diversionary force at Pensacola. (Jackson would return to Florida in the spring of 1818 and overwhelm both the Spanish and their allies, the Seminoles. "His invasion of Florida," it has been said, "convinced Madrid that this province . . . had better be sold before it was seized." [14] The following year Spain sold to the U.S. all the lands east of the Mississippi and all her claims to the Oregon country.)

After Horseshoe Bend and Pensacola, "Old Hickory"— ailing, anguished, indomitable—moved on to New Orleans where, on January 8, 1815, he and 3,500 of his back-country boys met 5,300 British soldiers commanded by Major General Sir Edward Pakenham. The battle left 2,000 British killed, wounded, or missing, with only 13 Americans killed and 58 wounded. And, ironically, all the bloodshed served no military purpose; the peace treaty between England and the U.S. had been signed at Ghent on Christmas Eve. But Jackson had won in an unforeseen way. New Orleans "made a future President of the United States, and in folklore wiped out all previous American defeats, ending the 'Second War of Independence' in a blaze of glory." [15]

Suddenly, from beyond the mountain barriers, there had appeared a threat to the Virginia dynasty. The "closed circle" atmosphere of that dynasty is suggested in a brief summary: "Virginia had supplied four of the five Presidents . . . Mr. Jefferson had been Secretary of State under President Washington. Mr. Madison had been Secretary of State under President Jefferson. Mr. Monroe had been Secretary of State under President

14. Samuel Eliot Morison, *The Oxford History of the American People* (New York: Oxford University Press, 1965), p. 410.

15. Morison, *Oxford History of the American People,* p. 395.

Madison. Mr. John Quincy Adams was Secretary of State under President Monroe.'' [16]

Virginia and New England had brought intellectual depth and diplomatic skill to the formation of the nation; now rude, vigorous, discontented men from the western regions, men who ''cared little for policies, but much for personality,'' thrust their first presidential candidate into the election of 1824. Jackson was defeated by one vote in the House of Representatives. But in the next election, 1828, Jackson won by 178 electoral votes to 83 for John Quincy Adams. He carried not only the South and the West, but Pennsylvania and most of New York, and this and the following election of 1832 proved that Jacksonian democracy was not so much a matter of state or region as of class. Jackson was the first president who had been born in a log cabin—and as one observer has commented, he made it well nigh impossible for anyone following him as a candidate who had *not* been born in a log cabin.

The ''common'' man saw many of his own characteristics intensified in Jackson's larger-than-life personality: instinct, more than intellect, shaped Jackson's responses to issues; he endured harsh physical pain from wounds received on the duelling ground and battlefield, and he suffered throughout the years of his presidency and until his own death over the loss of his Rachel a few weeks after his first election as president. He raced horses, fought cocks, resorted to law or pistols as the situation demanded, and spent a lifetime either stoking or banking the fires of feuds, personal and political. His administration introduced the ''spoils system''—or perhaps admitted its presence and sanctioned its practice—in government. But Jackson was so neglectful of ''spoils'' for himself that, when he left the White House, after two terms, his main possessions were a picture of Rachel and her Bible, ninety dollars in cash, the beautiful and spacious Hermitage he had built near Nashville, after New Orleans, and a cotton crop he would sell to meet debts incurred while he was president. When a New England historian later described him as ''one of nature's gentlemen,'' he was summariz-

16. G. W. Johnson, *Andrew Jackson,* p. 214.

ing what the general public had perceived in Jackson a century before: honesty, candor, courage, a character more complex than subtle, America's frontier nature personified.

Of Jackson's many confrontations and triumphs as president, two became particularly identified with his name: one involved the powerful Bank of the United States and its president, Nicholas Biddle, and the other pertained to a strategy called nullification and its proponent, John C. Calhoun. Nullification was the idea that the Union was a unit of states, of which each had the right to declare null and void any act of the federal government deemed a violation of the Constitution. Jackson was victorious in both struggles. Forthrightness was one of his weapons. Nowhere was it more evident than in the famous episode at the Jefferson Day banquet in the spring of 1830, when the powerful South Carolinian Calhoun and his followers hoped to trap Jackson into at least implied support of nullification. In the crowded banquet room of Washington's Indian Queen Hotel, there were twenty-four toasts, most of them either explicitly or implicitly favoring nullification and thereby dissolution of the Union. Then the president rose to his ramrod-straight six-feet-one, and beneath his thick brush of iron-grey hair the eyes as bright and fierce as an eagle's fixed on John Calhoun.

"Our Federal Union—it must be preserved!"

Only seven words, among the most important Old Hickory ever spoke. They carried a challenge that cut to the heart of a controversy bleeding at America's vitals.

During the next three troubled decades, the rare simplicity and vigor of the dauntless Tennessean who had fought throughout a lifetime for his state, his region, and, above all, his country, with every weapon at his command, would be diluted and virtually annulled—by the semantic and political skills of those who listened to the separatism of Jackson's mortal enemy, John C. Calhoun.

5

The Great Division

APRIL in Tennessee is the Canterbury pilgrims' season of sweet showers sung by Chaucer. It is the soggy earth of Shakespeare's *Tempest*. On occasion, as in the 1860s, it is also quite literally T. S. Eliot's cruellest month.

Spring spreads northward from the deep South, staining winter-brown fields and woods with varying shades of green. It flows up the mountainsides, opening delicate buds of trailing arbutus and trillium, "sarvis" shrubs, gaudy redbud and fragile silverbell. In April, the vague imprint of century-worn trenches at sites named Fort Pillow on the Mississippi, Fort Donelson on the Cumberland, Fort Sanders on a Knoxville hill above the Tennessee, are cushioned by greening sod. Grass covers the fertile pastures, so peaceful now, around Franklin and Murfreesboro. Along the rocky ribs of Cumberland Gap and Lookout Mountain, dogwoods whiten the rugged terrain with showers of spring snow. Even at Shiloh, terrible Shiloh, in a warm April noontime, there is the click and drone of beetles in the grass, bees among the early blossoms.

It began in April, that blood-letting called the Civil War, and it ended in April. During those four years between the spring of 1861 and 1865, some half a million Americans died of the soldierly pursuits of killing and attendant afflictions. It is impossible to estimate the numbers of unofficial casualties. And many of those who piled up on the battlefields and in the putrid hospitals were in Tennessee. From Big Creek in Hawkins County to Paris Landing in Henry County, 454 battles and skirmishes were waged in Tennessee. Only Virginia suffered more engagements on its soil.

Between the innocence of April '61 and the blood-bought knowledge of April '65, an estimated 100,000 to 135,000 Confederate Volunteers (their number exceeded by no other state) and between 35,000 and 50,000 Union Volunteers staked their all on the causes in which they believed. In addition, some 20,000 black Tennesseans were soldiers in the war. Tennessee could claim the highest percentage of Union casualties of any state.

Such statistics reflect the irreconcilable differences dividing a people; they do not reveal the anguish wrenching a family, the hate sundering a community, the loss impoverishing a region, as massive armies clashed by daylight and skulking raiders struck by night, destroying outright or slowly draining life from human and beast and earth alike.

The divisions were deep, part of that old geography reaching from level river plains to tilted mountain uplands. On the steep, uneven acres of East Tennessee, small farmers tilled their own holdings and larger landowners cultivated a variety of crops ranging from fruits and tobacco to the corn that made Tennessee at one time the leading "hog-and-hominy" state in the nation and the source of immense livestock drives to supply pork for single-crop planters of South Carolina and Georgia. On the wide, Black Belt bottomlands of West Tennessee, cotton plantations had developed by a labor system dependent on slavery.

Blacks were part of the earliest frontier in Tennessee. When Daniel Boone's son James was killed by Indians in the autumn of 1773, while hurrying to overtake his father and forty settlers on their way through Cumberland Gap, two Negro slaves who were with James escaped. Slaves were with John Donelson and James Robertson as they made their difficult journeys to establish Fort Nashborough. By the time of the first census in 1790, ten percent of all Tennesseans were Negroes. Being a border state influenced the development of Tennessee as a leading slave-trading state. The number of blacks increased dramat-

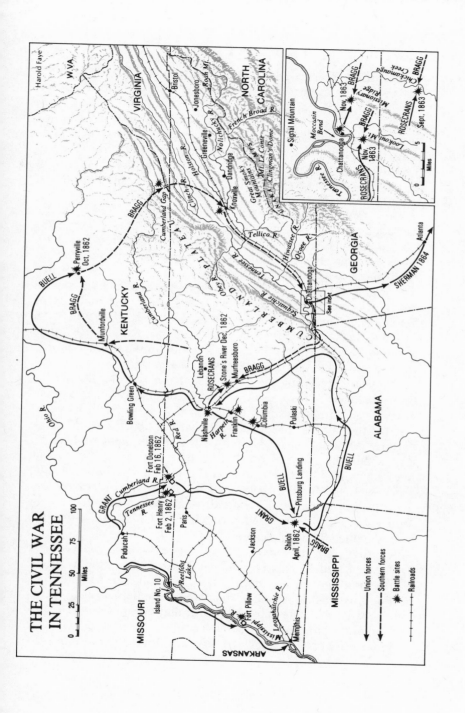

THE CIVIL WAR IN TENNESSEE

Harold Faye

Union forces
Southern forces
Battle sites
Railroads

Miles
0 25 50 75 100

W.VA.
VIRGINIA
NORTH CAROLINA
KENTUCKY
MISSOURI
ARKANSAS
MISSISSIPPI
ALABAMA
GEORGIA

Ohio R.
Paducah
Island No. 10
Fort Pillow
Memphis
Reelfoot Lake
Jackson
Paris
Tennessee R.
Fort Henry Feb 2, 1862
Fort Donelson Feb 16, 1862
Cumberland R.
Red R.
Loosahatchie R.
Wolf R.
Hatchie R.
Shiloh April, 1862
Pittsburg Landing
Bowling Green
Nashville
Harpeth R.
Franklin
Columbia
Pulaski
Lebanon
Murfreesboro
Stone's River Dec. 1862
ROSECRANS
BRAGG
GRANT
BUELL
Munfordville
Perryville Oct. 1862
BRAGG
BUELL
Cumberland Gap
CUMBERLAND PLATEAU
Cumberland R.
Obey R.
Sequatchie R.
Tennessee R.
Chattanooga
See inset
Clinch R.
Holston R.
Knoxville
Dandridge
Greeneville
Jonesboro
Bristol
Nolichucky R.
French Broad R.
Roan Mt.
Mt. Le Conte
Great Smoky Mountains
Clingman's Dome
Tellico R.
Hiwassee R.
Ocoee R.
Atlanta
SHERMAN 1864

Miles
0 5

Signal Mountain
Moccasin Bend
Tennessee R.
Chattanooga
Lookout Mt.
Missionary Ridge
Chickamauga Creek
ROSECRANS Sept. 1863
BRAGG
Nov 1863
BRAGG
Nov 1863
ROSECRANS

ically during the early decades of the nineteenth century until, just before the Civil War, slaves accounted for more than one fourth of the state's total population.

It was their distribution across the state that emphasized once more the inescapable influence of those three geographical divisions. Just prior to the war, a larger number of Negroes lived in the Bluegrass region of Middle Tennessee than anywhere else in the state—but a larger percentage (40 percent of the total population) lived in West Tennessee's cotton country.

As a contrast, mountainous East Tennessee counted among its people only 8 percent slaves and most of these were scattered along a half-dozen river valleys. Anywhere in the state, those vast Tara-like plantations of romantic fiction were rare. In 1860, there were only 47 slaveholders in Tennessee who owned more than 100 slaves; 7,614 held between four and six slaves; the largest number—7,820—owned one slave; the majority of Tennesseans owned no slaves at all. But out of the national struggle over slavery and the fundamental dispute over state sovereignty had arisen side issues and emotions sufficient to fuel four years of war and generations of rancor.

The years preceding the Civil War, from 1836 to 1856, have been characterized as decades of "partisan fury." At the national level, Tennesseans joined Texans in waging successful war for the latter's independence from Mexico; James K. Polk became president of the United States and brought more territory within the national boundaries than any other first executive, including Jefferson and his Louisiana Purchase. At the state level, the forced removal of the Cherokee Indians, under the direction of General Winfield Scott, began in stockades in Tennessee and Georgia and proceeded to Oklahoma along the death-haunted Trail of Tears.

The first train in Tennessee made its exhibition run between La Grange and Memphis; a Great Western and Southwestern Convention held in Memphis boosted enthusiasm for rail connections between Tennessee and other Southern states. Nashville became the state capital. And in that city, a Southern convention devoted a nine-day session to discussion of slavery.

Andrew Johnson was elected governor in 1855. Emotions in-

TENNESSEE

A photographer's essay by Joe Clark, HBSS

tensified, as events seemed to gather momentum in pushing people and leaders alike into polarized, unalterable stands on the twin issues of slavery and union. Personal confrontations multiplied. Editors shot one another over accusations of abolitionism. Tennessee students at the University of Pennsylvania transferred to the University of Nashville when a professor suggested, after the Harpers Ferry raid, that John Brown's death penalty might be too harsh. A hapless fruit-tree salesman from Ohio was suspected of being an abolitionist and was arrested in Knoxville on no apparent charge. When citizens at his trial differed over the truth of his testimony and the verdict as to his immediate future, sticks and pistols were brought into the deliberations. Eventually, the terrified stranger was allowed to flee the agitated town.

If passions favoring the South were strong, so too were those holding with Union. Elected Tennessee's governor in 1857 and 1859, Isham G. Harris was a strong Southern sympathizer; yet, when he and the Tennessee General Assembly called early in 1861 for a statewide vote on a convention to determine the state's relationship to the federal government, the move was defeated, 69,387 to 57,798. Unionists claimed a significant victory. Those who followed Old Hickory's devotion—"Our Federal Union, it must be preserved!"—were not voting directly on the issue of slavery. In fact, many of them feared the competition of free black labor. But they were committed to continuation of the united United States.

In April, however, Fort Sumter was fired upon. President Lincoln issued a call for troops. Governor Harris answered the call: "Tennessee will not furnish a single man for purposes of coercion, but 50,000 if necessary for the defense of our rights and those of our Southern brothers." [1] The state was rent by argument and difference.

In typical Tennessee style, the referendum held on June 8 to determine what course the state should follow was no simple secession measure. It was described as the vote on a measure to

1. Stanley F. Horn, *The Army of the Tennessee* (Indianapolis: Bobbs-Merrill, 1941), p. 47.

reassert Tennessee's sovereignty and declare her independence from the United States. The declaration of independence from the union and representation in the Confederacy was favored by a majority of 104,913 to 47,238. There remained, however, Tennesseans unwilling to abide by this decision, and they proposed their own secession movement.

Nine days after the statewide vote, delegates from twenty-six East Tennessee counties met in Greeneville and petitioned the legislature to allow them to form a separate state. Governor Harris, now himself a "Rebel" governor, deplored East Tennesseans "bent on rebellion."

The little secession within the big secession was never formally declared. But co-operation between Unionist East Tennesseans and the rest of the state never became a reality. Throughout the war, this divided citizenry engaged in struggle at two levels. One was on the designated battlefields; the other, more hidden but no less fervent, flared in homes, crossroads, villages, and cities, wherever people carried on their daily pursuits and came in contact with those holding opposite opinions. Much of the severity of the Reconstruction period following the war could be traced to the resentment and revenge kindled by these home-front hostilities.

Although the Unionist counties never succeeded in accomplishing their break from the Confederacy, individuals in large numbers carried on their own secession. Singly and in squads, they crossed into Kentucky, many to Camp Dick Robinson, where they could enlist in the U.S. Army. By October 1861, one agitated resident of Knoxville could write to Governor Harris that he was satisfied Lincoln had more East Tennessee followers than did Confederate General Felix Zollicoffer. "There is no giving way in the hostile feelings in East Tennessee." [2] In fact, President Lincoln also was aware of the widespread Unionist loyalty in East Tennessee and urged all possible support for these citizens.

In November, a citizen of Jonesboro wrote to Confederate

2. *A History of Tennessee from the Earliest Times to the Present,* 6. vols. (Nashville: Goodspeed Publishing Co., 1886, 1887), p. 484.

President Jefferson Davis that "Civil war has broken out at length in East Tennessee." [3] The end of hostilities was not in sight unless "the Union element" could be expatriated, once and for all.

No one was expatriated, but many on each side were ambushed, robbed, and subjected to mounting fury as the war dragged on. Added to the partisan bitterness of the home-front war in the Eastern part of the state was the marauding theft and murder inflicted by the outliers. These were men who "lay out" from serving any cause but their own. Joining with bushwhackers, with guerilla bands of plunderers and scavengers, the outliers looted homes and farms and businesses of Unionist and Confederate alike. They grew bolder as the war intensified, and their depredations infested all parts of the state. After the first flush of confidence and enthusiasm, as the realities of war became ever more grimly apparent, desertions from both armies multiplied. Sometimes these deserters, when captured, boasted that they had taken an oath of allegiance only "from the teeth out."

As the war began, one Confederate attitude toward the Tennessee mountain area was reflected in an account by a Southern historian who described the abundance of its hills, rocks, poverty, and ignorance, while conceding that, militarily, it was of great importance to the Confederacy. Indeed, in a less derogatory tone, the *Richmond* (Va.) *Enquirer* had spoken of East Tennessee as the "keystone of the Southern arch." [4]

Geography made it that keystone. Most of the crucial Western campaign in the Civil War was waged for control of rivers or railroads, and Tennessee was central to that strategy. The Cumberland and the Tennessee, along with the Mississippi, were indispensable arteries of commerce, while Tennessee railroads were central to the network connecting Atlantic Coast and Deep South, border states and the Gulf.

Cumberland Gap, a narrow defile through the mountain

3. Goodspeed, *History of Tennessee,* p. 486.

4. Digby G. Seymour, *Divided Loyalties* (Knoxville: University of Tennessee Press, 1963).

barrier sixty miles north of Knoxville, controlled access to the valley of East Tennessee. The Gap was also a gateway through which East Tennessee Union sympathizers poured north to enlist in the United States camps in Kentucky. Throughout the war, control of this picturesque passage seesawed from Confederates under Zollicoffer to Federals under G. W. Morgan to Confederates under Bragg to Federals under Burnside—and became a critical factor in larger decisive campaigns to the south.

The Gap was also a symbol; as George Morgan's Tennessee troops in blue retreated before Bragg's men in grey in October 1862, there were tears in their eyes. For their part, some of the approaching Confederate troops—forced to forage for food on their advance march—squeezed humor out of their hardship in the mountains by wondering if C.S.A. no longer stood for Confederate States of America, but for *Corn, Salt* and *Apples*—part of their survival.

Those who hoped for peaceful coexistence at home between the state's partisans had their optimism shattered, early on. The catalyst was a dramatic episode that permanently polarized allegiances and released the first shock waves of fear and retaliation. During the chilly night of November 8, 1861, a small band of East Tennessee Unionists, acting with the approval of President Lincoln and General McClellan, burned five key wooden railroad bridges south of the Virginia border in Tennessee. Attempts on four others failed. News of the burned bridges spread like leaf-fire across the state and to the capitals of Washington and Richmond. Reaction flamed out of all proportion to the event. Martial law was imposed, those accused of Union sympathies were jailed in Knoxville at the rate of fifteen to sixty suspects a day; alarums of invasion and rumors of uprisings multiplied as the heat of emotion overwhelmed the light of reality. Confederate Secretary of War Judah Benjamin issued orders that those identified with the bridge burnings "are to be tried summarily by drum-head court-martial, and, if found guilty, executed on the spot by hanging. It would be well to leave their bodies hanging in the vicinity of the burned bridges." [5]

5. Oliver P. Temple, *East Tennessee and the Civil War* (Cincinnati: R. Clarke, 1899), p. 392.

Five who were captured were quickly executed; the bodies of two of them were left hanging near the railroad track for four days, as a warning to their sympathizers and a source of satisfaction to their enemies.

Decomposing bodies swinging beside a public thoroughfare were only a harbinger of the full horror of the years to follow. Three months after the bridge burnings, in February 1862, Fort Henry on the Tennessee River and Fort Donelson on the Cumberland fell before attacks of U. S. Grant, who coined here a lasting watchword for his strategy and a nickname for himself: Unconditional Surrender. More than 14,000 Confederates did surrender in this initial drive to divide the South. Nashville, at mid-century the largest city in the state, was abandoned in the flight of most of its 10,000 citizens, as General Don Carlos Buell and his Federal troops moved in, and Andrew Johnson was made Military Governor of Tennessee.

Spring of 1862 arrived, and on a balmy Sunday morning in April, five Union divisions under General Grant enjoyed the lazy warmth of the sunshine pouring over their encampment in the vicinity of Shiloh Church, near Pittsburg Landing on the Tennessee River. A soldier later remembered the leisure and beauty of that warm, cloudless morning:

> The boys were scattered around the company streets and in front of the company parade grounds, engaged in polishing and brightening their muskets, and brushing up and cleaning their shoes, jackets, trousers, and clothing generally . . .
>
> The morning was strangely still. The wagons were silent, the mules were peacefully munching their hay, and the army teamsters were giving us a rest. I listened with delight to the plaintive, mournful tones of a turtle-dove in the woods close by, while on a dead limb of a tall tree right in the camp a wood-pecker was sounding his "long roll." [6]

Suddenly, in the distance, "came a dull, heavy 'Pum!,' then another, and still another. Every man sprung to his feet as if struck by an electric shock, and we looked inquiringly into one another's faces." The ominous growl became a low, sullen

---

6. Henry Steele Commager, *The Blue and the Gray* (Indianapolis: Bobbs-Merrill, 1950), p. 359.

roar; "it was the continuous roll of thousands of muskets, and told us that a battle was on." [7]

Shiloh was its name. General Albert Sidney Johnston had promised his attacking Confederate troops that they would water their horses that night in the Tennessee River. Startled Union pickets ran to report to their superiors that "the Johnnies are thicker than Spanish needles in a fence corner." [8]

Grant's army reeled under the surprise and strength of the attack; fleeing soldiers sought shelter under the bluffs along the river; a private who had been at Fort Donelson helped nervous recruits with their weapons and reassured them: "Why, it's just like shooting squirrels, only these squirrels have guns, that's all." The guns took their toll throughout the long, confused, terrible day. At a place called the Peach Orchard, hails of bullets cut the petals from the blossoming trees until they "floated down on the firing line like a gentle pink rain." [9]

There was a little stronghold the Confederates named "the Hornet's Nest," where all count was lost of the toll of Union dead. At the Hornet's Nest, Albert Sidney Johnston—considered by Jefferson Davis the greatest soldier then living—suffered a severed artery in the thigh and died while Tennessee's Governor Isham Harris, who had been riding beside him, tried to stanch the gushing blood.

At the end of the day, the Confederates were in control—but Grant was still there. And Buell had pushed down from Nashville with re-enforcements to help the demoralized federal troops. General Pierre Beauregard replaced the fallen Johnston in Confederate command; but by the second day, momentum and strength had shifted to the Union side. During the night, it had rained—the dead, the dying, the wounded, thousands of them, lay amidst the greening Tennessee woodlands and fields, and the April rain drenched blue and gray uniforms with equal blessing or misery.

7. Commager, *The Blue and the Gray,* p. 359.
8. Commager, *The Blue and the Gray,* p. 361.
9. Bruce Catton, *This Hallowed Ground* (New York: Doubleday, 1956), pp. 114, 115.

By midafternoon on Monday, Beauregard was withdrawing, taking his battered army south to Corinth, Mississippi. Grant and his battered army remained on the field. The costly casualties on both sides had been remarkably close in number: 1,754 Federals killed and 8,408 wounded; 1,723 Confederates killed, 8,012 wounded.

Shiloh was a decisive engagement. It tilted the balance that the Confederacy would never regain in the Mississippi Valley region. It revealed the murderous ferocity at the heart of the war. And, as historian Bruce Catton has pointed out,

> It had been possible, before, for a Northerner or a Southerner to believe that the other side was really not very much in earnest and would presently give up. Grant had had that delusion before Shiloh; so, perhaps, had Johnston, who whistled his men north from Corinth with contemptuous remarks about "agrarian mercenaries" in the northern army. After Shiloh no intelligent man could feel as Grant and Johnston had felt. For Shiloh underlined one of the basic facts about the war—that it was being fought by men of enormous innate pugnacity; tenacious men who would quit a fight once begun only when someone was *beaten*. [10]

After the bloodletting at Shiloh, the chase of the locomotive known as *The General*—between Kennesaw, Georgia, and Chattanooga—which occurred a few days later, on April 12, seemed like a diverting joy-ride.

A Union spy, James J. Andrews, and twenty cohorts, in an effort to isolate Chattanooga, undertook to capture a train and burn bridges on railroads between Tennessee and Georgia. They captured *The General* and three boxcars at Kennesaw Station, Georgia, and headed north, pursued by two dauntless trainmen. As Andrews and his men cut telegraph wires and piled crossties on the track behind them, the pursuers commandeered handcars, other engines, and telegraph facilities. When the pirated locomotive ran out of fuel, the raiders fled, but all were soon captured. In Chattanooga, Andrews and seven of his train-nappers were tried and executed. Others were eventually transferred or escaped—and six who were finally paroled became the first re-

10. Catton, *This Hallowed Ground*, p. 120.

cipients of the nation's highest award, the Medal of Honor. In a later century, Tennessee and Georgia would engage in heated dispute over the final resting place of *The General*.

In June 1862, Union forces captured Memphis, with its important cotton market. The city of around 9,000 people was a stepping-stone toward Vicksburg and New Orleans.

Throughout that summer, two of the South's most dashing cavalrymen—Nathan Bedford Forrest and John Hunt Morgan—harassed federal forces throughout Middle Tennessee. Their daring and success lifted Confederate morale. Perhaps few men represented more completely than this native Tennessean, Nathan Bedford Forrest, much of the strength and weakness of the Southern cause. At the time he enlisted, Forrest was a wealthy trader in cotton, livestock, real estate—and slaves. Described as tall, lithe, and of commanding presence, he had risen from a background of poverty and scanty education to become a self-made millionaire, and he brought to the war a native ability to lead. Fellow officers spoke of his military genius; superiors and subordinates alike encountered his violent temper; the enemy called him "that devil Forrest"; his men followed as he fulfilled his simple and famous maxim to "get there first with the most," or—as popular idiom had it—"fustest with the mostest." Historians have concluded that he had a more modern conception of logistics than most West Point officers.

Controversy surrounded Forrest. When Union-held Fort Pillow in Tennessee, manned by 262 Negro and 295 white troops, surrendered under Forrest's attack on April 12, 1864, was there a massacre, or were the disproportionate federal casualties all the result of battle? When Forrest joined the newly formed Ku Klux Klan, following the war, did he act justifiably as its Grand Wizard and condone its lawless practices? Reverberations of thundering hoofs on his swift successful cavalry strikes mingle with the chant of the slave trader, the questions surrounding massacre and Klan, to echo down the corridors of history.

While the flexible, hard-hitting cavalry of Forrest and Morgan and General Joseph Wheeler struck, destroyed the enemy's supplies, withdrew, and reappeared on another front, the armies met in more ponderous struggle. The Confederates thrust northward into Kentucky, then fell back to Middle Tennessee where, on the last day of December 1862, the Union Army of the Cumberland, under General William S. Rosecrans, and the Confederate Army of Tennessee, under General Braxton Bragg, met at Murfreesboro—or Stone's River, as the engagement was named. Three days of fighting left a harvest of almost 3,000 dead and more than 15,000 wounded on both sides—and a result described as "tactical victory" and "strategic defeat" for the Confederates. Whatever the terminology, Bragg withdrew— and went into winter quarters in Bedford and Coffee counties.

The year 1863 arrived, the year of Chancellorsville, "Robert E. Lee's masterpiece," with its irreplaceable loss of Stonewall Jackson; of Vicksburg in the west and Gettysburg in the east; and in Tennessee a steady, costly accumulation of battles. In September, Burnside occupied Knoxville and found crowds along the streets welcoming his Union troops, while Bragg and Longstreet and Hood moved against Rosecrans and George H. Thomas, and, after one of the bloodiest days of the entire war, won a victory at Chickamauga.

But Bragg failed to seize his advantage, and dissatisfaction raged among his officers and men. Rosecrans was locked in Chattanooga, but Bragg did not attack: he laid siege. And he made a disastrous mistake. He ordered Longstreet, with 15,000 veteran troops, away from Chattanooga to attack Burnside at Knoxville.

As opposition, Bragg now faced George H. Thomas, Rosecrans's replacement as commander of the U.S. Army of the Cumberland. The tenacity that would soon win Thomas fame as "the Rock of Chickamauga" was indicated by his assertion that he would hold Chattanooga until starvation. Bragg remained a favorite of President Jefferson Davis, if not of his men; and despite deep-seated discontent, he remained in command. When the forces of Bragg and Thomas finally met, November 23–24, in the "Battle above the Clouds," shrouded by fog and mist on the steep slopes of Lookout Mountain, the Confederates were driven from the stronghold.

And on November 25, along the 500-foot height of Missionary Ridge, an incredible event occurred. There had been no

plan for the Union Army of the Cumberland to take the ridge itself. The trenches at its base were the target. But when four infantry divisions—18,000 men in blue—began to move, in a line
two miles wide, their momentum gathered power. Under fire
from guns above them, they went through the first line of
trenches and simply stormed up the mountain. Grant and
Thomas, watching at a distance, could not believe what they
beheld. Individually and in groups, fighting hand-to-hand, the
Federals swarmed up the steep slope, as Confederate forces
abandoned the summit. It was the end of the Chattanooga campaign. The Confederacy had met another severe loss.

The panic and turmoil of civilian life caught in war's up-
heaval was described by the famous newspaperman, Charles A.
Dana, who was also U.S. Assistant Secretary of War visiting
Chattanooga at the time of the battle. He wrote:

> I rode twelve miles to Chattanooga, galloping my horse all the way,
> to send dispatches to Washington, and found the road filled all the
> distance with baggage-wagons, artillery, ambulances, negros on
> horseback, field and company officers, wounded men limping
> along, Union refugees from the country around leading their wives
> and children, mules running along loose, squads of cavalry—in
> short, every element that could confuse the rout of a great army, not
> excepting a major-general commanding an army corps.[11]

The result of this campaign left the way open to Atlanta and
eventually to Sherman's march to the sea. Four days after Missionary Ridge, on November 29, Longstreet attacked Burnside
in Knoxville after a bitterly cold night of frozen sleet. He lost
the battle of Fort Sanders and led his weary Confederate troops
into winter quarters in the valley of East Tennessee, where
pumpkins and corn were still in the fields for foraging. Before
the winter was over, the men's bare feet would leave blood-
stains on the snow covering sharp-rutted roads. The general who
had sent Longstreet on this mission, Braxton Bragg, was finally
replaced on December 1 by Joseph E. Johnston—but too late.
The war was being lost by the South in the West—and Tennessee was part of both that South and that West.

Events of 1864 marched with growing certainty toward one conclusion—not visible, then, of course, in the savage spring-time battles of the Wilderness in Virginia and Spotsylvania Court House and Cold Harbor, and summer's siege of Atlanta and Sherman's winter march to the sea, but becoming ever more apparent, more inescapable. In November and December, at Franklin and Nashville, the final desperate battles were waged in Tennessee, with costly Confederate defeats. By the time the Army of Tennessee joined Confederate forces in North Carolina to surrender to Sherman in April 1865, it had dwindled to a force of only some 5,000 men.

The condition of that force at an earlier time was suggested in a single description by an Ohio recruit who walked along the fighting line at one end of Missionary Ridge the day after that battle. Bruce Catton reports the Federal soldier's words as he looked at the corpse of an unburied Confederate on the Tennessee mountain:

> He was not over 15 years of age, and very slender in size. He was clothed in a cotton suit, and was barefooted—barefooted, on that cold and wet 24th of November. I examined his haversack. For a day's ration there was a handful of black beans, a few pieces of sorghum and a half dozen roasted acorns. That was an infinitely poor outfit for marching and fighting, but that Tennessee Confederate had made it answer his purpose.[12]

Suffering and death took their toll, not only on the battlefield, but in hospital and camp, as well. One young soldier who survived the onslaught of Missionary Ridge was unnerved when he came upon a haystack pile of arms and legs removed by surgeons following that engagement. For decades to come, youngsters growing up in villages of the Delta and the Midwest, cities of New England and the South, would encounter aging men whose missing legs or arms or eyes were reminders of the tolls of war.

And the deadliest enemy of every soldier was not his counterpart in uniform, but disease. One Confederate medical authority believed that disease killed three Confederate soldiers for every

---

12. Catton, *This Hallowed Ground,* p. 303.

one killed in battle. Chief among the killers were measles, malaria, smallpox, typhoid fever—and, most common, dysentery and diarrhea. Care of the sick and wounded was primitive, indifferent. In Murfreesboro, a young woman found dying men at the soldier's hospital with no more notice taken of them than if they had been dogs. Common medicines included whiskey, turpentine, opium, quinine, calomel. Since the germ theory was not yet accepted, sterilization was unknown. One rusty, germ-ridden knife in an overworked surgeon's hand could dispense with more lives than many a young private wielding his bayonet at Franklin or in defense of Fort Sanders.

Small irritations often developed into major disasters. Commonplace blisters could become hellish sources of pain during long marches. One soldier on the Western front vowed that he had had them "one under the other, on the heel, behind the heel, on the ball of the foot, on every toe, a network, a labyrinth, an archipelago of agony." He was sure that other afflictions, such as heat, hunger, and thirst, were minor when compared with such torment. A whole regiment could turn "nearly mutinous with suffering." [13]

As they crossed and re-crossed Tennessee, the armies made a heavy impact on the countryside. Woodlands were laid waste during their encampments. Row after row of fence rails disappeared; one soldier in Sequatchie Valley estimated that, during one interval, his men had burned enough rails in that place "to fence an entire county." [14] Crops in the fields were stolen or destroyed, barns were plundered, food was snatched from smokehouse, bin, or barrel. Most devastating of all, the animals that were essential to each farm's survival were drafted for army use.

Civil War soldiers on their horses and mules influenced all aspects of civilian life. One of the most vivid descriptions of the movements of men and animals across the bleak winter landscape of Tennessee is that written by General E. P. Alexander,

13. Commager, *The Blue and the Gray*, p. 422.

14. J. Leonard Raulston and James W. Livingood, *Sequatchie* (Knoxville: University of Tennessee Press, 1974), p. 155.

serving as General Longstreet's artillery chief in late 1864, when Confederate forces were moving northward from Knoxville, seeking winter quarters. "The roads were in fearful condition," he wrote,

and in the inky darkness and pouring rain neither men nor animals could see. Frequently guns or wagons would be mired so that the column behind would be blocked in the mud until extra teams and men at the wheels could set the column going for a few minutes. Strict orders had been given that the men should not use fence rails for fuel, but that night the orders were ignored, and miles of fence were fired merely to light up the road . . .

We were so badly off for horse-shoes that on the advance to Knoxville we had stripped the shoes from all the dead horses, and we killed for the purpose all the wounded and broken-down animals, both our own and those left behind by the enemy. During the siege the river brought down to us a number of dead horses and mules, thrown in within the town. We watched for them, took them out, and got the shoes and nails from their feet. Our men were nearly as badly off as the animals—perhaps worse, as they did not have hoofs. I have myself seen bloody stains on frozen ground, left by the bare-footed where our infantry had passed. We of the artillery took the shoes off the drivers and gave them to the cannoneers who had to march.[15]

After settling in near Morristown, the army found food in the fields and livestock in the barns, but they could not escape the need for protection of their feet. "For shoes," General Alexander said, "we were obliged to resort to the raw hides of beef cattle as temporary protection from the frozen ground. Then we began to find soldiers who could tan the hides of our beeves, some who could make shoes, some who could make shoe-pegs, some who could make shoe-lasts, so that it came about that the hides passed rapidly from the beeves to the feet of the soldiers." [16]

If the gruelling marches and battles were harsh, equally hard

15. Stanley F. Horn, editor, *Tennessee's War* (Nashville: Tennessee Civil War Centennial Commission, 1965), p. 245.

16. Horn, editor, *Tennessee's War*, p. 246.

to endure were the long encampments and their boredom. In winter quarters across Tennessee, or awaiting final orders for attack, the soldiers drank and smoked and gambled and found women who would help them forget that war was tedious more often than it was glorious. They read their Bibles and on occasion participated in wholesale religious revivals. They bought watches from traveling peddlers, had their pictures made by itinerant photographers, swapped trophies and tall tales. Their diversions were often simple, rustic in the tradition of their forefathers. A soldier in the Army of Tennessee recorded that among his friends were some of the finest mimics in the world. "Let one cackle like a hen, and the monotony of camp is broken by the encore of 'Shoo- o -!' Then other cackles take it up, until it sounds like a poultry yard stirred up over a mink or a weasel. Let one bray like an ass, others take it up until the whole regiment will personate the sound, seemingly like a fair ground of asses." [17]

The cook accompanying one general took a pet rooster named "Old Dick" through all their campaigns in Tennessee and neighboring states, and "Old Dick" won fifty campaigns of his own in as many cock-fights.

During the years of Civil War in Tennessee, knaves and heroes emerged from unlikely sources, and the state gave leaders both renowned and anonymous to both sides of the conflict. In addition to those already mentioned, there was David Farragut, hill-bound Knox County's son, who became the highest-ranking officer in the U.S. Navy and assured Mobile Bay a place in memory when he commanded, "Damn the torpedoes! Full steam ahead!" In 1866, he became the first full admiral in the nation's history. And there was a young Confederate boy hanged near Pulaski when he would not reveal the name of the spy who had given him information about Federal troops: Sam Davis's own name was listed in the annals of bravery.

There was Dan Ellis, in Carter County, known as the "Red Fox," one of the pilots for either East Tennesseans fleeing Confederate conscription or captured Federal soldiers escaping from

17. Commager, *The Blue and the Gray*, p. 440.

Deep South prisons. Ellis's intimate knowledge of the mountain ranges, their hidden valleys and passes, and his cool courage under pressure made him a valuable ally. He kept no formal record of the numbers of Tennessee Unionists he piloted to Camp Dick Robinson and similar federal installations in Kentucky; there was no list of the gaunt, fearful escapees who tapped on his door at night and asked his help in finding their way north to home. His effectiveness was best reflected, perhaps, in the fact that, before the end of the War, the Confederate government placed a standing offer of five thousand dollars on Dan Ellis's head.

And along the southeastern border of the state, there was the Thomas Legion, recruited in 1862 by W. H. Thomas, a North Carolina trader adopted into the Cherokee tribe when he was a boy, later becoming chief agent for the eastern Cherokees. In 1861, as a member of the North Carolina legislature, Thomas was a strong Confederate, and the Cherokees followed his leadership. When he formed the Thomas Legion, four companies were made up of his Cherokee friends—some 400 of them, almost every able-bodied man in the eastern band. Thomas stated that his main object was to keep the Cherokees out of the path of the large armies and use them as scouts and home guards through the mountains along the North Carolina-Tennessee border. There were scattered raids and skirmishes between mountain Unionists, Federal troops led by Col. George W. Kirk, and the Confederate Cherokees. Construction on a road across the Great Smoky Mountains was begun under General Thomas's supervision. But the main Confederate forces retreated from East Tennessee in the dark winter of 1863–1864, and the Cherokees left the area, too, returning to their farms and woodlands on the North Carolina side of the mountains.

Battles had been fought with words as well as bullets. In Knoxville, Whig editor William G. Brownlow attacked secession and its advocates with such bile and vigor that he was forced to flee to the foothills of the Smokies in nearby Sevier County and hide there with friends. After later suffering imprisonment in the Knoxville jail, he went North, where he began a series of highly successful lecture tours describing the infamies of the Confederacy, raising funds for Tennessee Unionists. On the opposite side, in mid-1862, when Memphis fell to federal control, the editor-publisher of the *Memphis Appeal* fled south to Mississippi. His paper did not miss a single issue and continued proclaiming its strong Confederate sympathies.

Despite accumulating enmities and tensions, there were interludes of tolerance and pleasantry that made life endurable. In February 1863, a wedding on Walden's Ridge near Chattanooga was celebrated by an all-night dance later remembered by a participant:

> I do not suppose that the world contains such a rare case of universal *concord* being the result of universal *discord*. The party was composed of 1st, Rebel and Union citizens; 2d, Rebel and Union soldiers; 3rd, Rebel and Union deserters; 4th, Rebel and Union spies; 5th, Rebel and Union bushwhackers.
>
> Scarcely a harsh word was uttered during the whole night; all danced together as if nothing was wrong, and parted mutually the next morning, each party marching off separately.[18]

Bloodshed was more often the rule of life in Tennessee during those years. Bushwhackers infested ever larger areas of the state. By early 1865, officers stationed at Cumberland Gap were following orders "to shoot a guerilla whenever and wherever he is found, and not to take prisoners on any account."[19] At Athens, guerilla raiders were pursued—five were killed, fifteen horses, two rifles, two carbines, and two fine pistols captured. In Tullahoma, an officer discovered that "many of the very worst bushwackers were boys between the ages of fourteen and eighteen."[20]

Travelers often tried to avoid the mountains of Tennessee because of increasing danger of being attacked by outliers, singly or in gangs. Even with the close of the war, hostilities did not end. Revenge took many forms, from murder to a dousing in honey for a man who had guided foragers during the war to his neighbors' corn-cribs and beehives.

---

18. Govan and Livingood, *Chattanooga Country*, p. 207.

19. *Official Records of the War of the Rebellion*, series I, vol. XLIX, part I (Washington, D.C.: U.S. Government Printing Office, 1889), p. 9.

20. *Official Records of the War of the Rebellion*, series I, vol. XLIX, part II, p. 291.

The division which East Tennessean J. G. M. Ramsey had said made the state essentially two people, which West Tennessean Nathan Bedford Forrest had warned would "bust hell wide open," was settled—at least on the battlefield. Appomattox brought an end to war in the United States and in Tennessee. It did not bring peace.

Memories would fester for generations to come, as exemplified by Captain R. A. Ragan, who fled his home in Cocke County to join the Union army in Kentucky in 1863. He and the friends who accompanied him reached the top of the Cumberland Mountain in sad condition, and Ragan later wrote: "James H. Randolph of Newport, Tennessee, was with us. I was sorry for him as well as the others. His shoes were entirely worn out and his feet were bleeding. I can remember the circumstances as though it were but a few days ago. He looked at me and said, 'Bob, when we get back to Tennessee we will give them H_____ and rub it in.' " [21]

For four years, Tennessee had been at the center of the nation's cruellest testing. Roads had deteriorated under steady use by armies of men and animals. Railroads had been wrenched from their beds. Farms had been laid waste, some burned and abandoned. Thousands of freedmen seeking a new way of life crowded into towns and cities.

The well-known writer, John T. Trowbridge, touring the South in the year following the end of the war, found a variety of conditions and surprises in Tennessee: President Andrew Johnson's brick home in Greeneville was the victim of Confederate vandalism, smallpox raged among the black population in Chattanooga, Nashville boasted the finest State Capitol in the nation, and Memphis impressively combined beautiful situation and commercial activity.

Tennessee had survived a brutal war on its soil and a slaughter among its people. Time, energy, financial resources, vision—and luck—would be required to heal the wounds inflicted by fratricidal conflict. Among the people offering these necessities were a number of newcomers. Many of them had seen Ten-

---

21. Ruth Webb O'Dell, *Over the Misty Blue Hills: The Story of Cocke County, Tennessee* (Newport: privately printed, 1951), p. 334.

nessee first while they were serving in the army. They returned, after the war, to settle in a locale they found attractive. Chattanooga enjoyed a significant number of such citizens and encouraged their immigration. General John T. Wilder exemplified the best among them. During the Chattanooga campaign, Wilder had commanded an Indiana brigade and observed the potential of the region. He returned, to start making iron with coke. With a group of associates, he founded the Roane Iron Company at Rockwood, mining coal, operating coke ovens and pig-iron furnaces. Later, he built a sprawling, unique hostelry, the Cloudland Hotel, atop Roan Mountain in the northeastern corner of the state.

Today, on two small segments of lawn in front of the courthouse at Greeneville, Tennessee, stand two historical markers. One memorial says, in part:

General John H. Morgan 1825–1864
"The Thunderbolt of the Confederacy"

His command, never exceeding 4,000 men, was composed
largely of Kentuckians and Tenneseeans. It was renowned
for boldness and celerity on raid, carrying terror
into the region north of the Ohio.
The "Great Raider" was surprised at night
and killed by a detachment of the command
of Gen. A. C. Gillem on the premises
of the Williams home near this spot on Sept 4, 1864.

His heroism is in the heritage of the South.

The opposite shaft has a quite different commemoration. On its west side are the words:

To the memory of the Union Soldiers who enlisted in
Union Army from Greene County, War 1861–1865

And on the south side:

In the hour of their country's peril
they were loyal and true

This may be the only county seat in the United States that offers, side by side, monuments honoring both the Union and the

Confederate causes in the Civil War. Those markers represent the four long, wounding years of a conflict that, in Tennessee, was truly a "brother's war."

At its close, Tennessee had left behind forever the first harsh frontier of natural wilderness and the bloody frontier of that collective morality which pledged one nation indivisible, securing to all persons freedom, justice, and equality of opportunity for pursuit of happiness. The frontier spirit remained. It was the nature and scope of the challenge that changed.

6

Wars of Roses and
Ballot Boxes

ATTLE in the fields and towns was over, but another warfare raged, one with which Tennesseans were thoroughly familiar. It substituted ballots for bullets and oratory for sharpshooters, but the history of political contest in the state has shown it often to be kissing-cousin to military conflict.

It is necessary to remember, however, that one of the select company of Americans ever to receive the Nobel Peace Prize was a Tennessean who grew up in the years following the Civil War. Cordell Hull, born in Overton County in 1871, reared in the Obed and Wolf River area, drew on some of the Reconstruction resources of his rural neighborhood to shape attitudes and insights that would make him one of the nation's twentieth-century statesmen.

In later life, Cordell Hull recalled not only the hardships and privations of Reconstruction, but the privileges, as well. From lively debates and discussions among "old soldiers congregated inside and outside the little country stores, on rainy days or on Saturday afternoons," he learned much about "the big vital questions of government." Central to this experience was "the whole doctrine and spirit of individual liberty." [1]

1. Cordell Hull, with Andrew H. T. Berding, *The Memoirs of Cordell Hull* (New York: Macmillan, 1948), 1:16.

He became U.S. Congressman, Senator, and finally Secretary of State under President Franklin D. Roosevelt. Hull won international respect and renown, especially for his efforts to achieve a strong Good Neighbor Policy among the twenty-one American republics and to create an effective United Nations organization. In 1945, he was awarded the Nobel Peace Prize.

Cordell Hull drew lessons for peace from memories of Civil War. Perhaps his antithesis was the man who became governor of Tennessee during the fateful years of Reconstruction—a man who, symbolically and literally, perpetuated much of the bitterness that carried over from battlefield to campaign trail and voting booth.

"Parson" William Gannaway Brownlow had enjoyed a turbulent career as Methodist circuit rider, writer, and newspaper editor before he plunged into politics. His religious exhortations were warmed by denunciation more often than they were lighted by annunciation, and his purpose frequently seemed to be controversy more than conversion. He rode the Southern highlands and edited the *Knoxville Whig,* fighting the enemies of the Lord, who also happened to be his own adversaries: the devil, Baptists, Presbyterians, Democrats, and finally Confederates, possibly in ascending order of their error.

His allegiances were reflected in the degrees of his belligerence. He believed in the federal government and therefore hated its opponents: "I expect to stand by this Union, and battle to sustain it, though Whiggery and Democracy, Slavery and Abolitionism, Southern rights and Northern wrongs, are all blown to the devil!" He also believed in slavery and therefore hated Harriet Beecher Stowe: "She is as ugly as Original sin—an abomination in the eyes of civilized people." When the rumor was spread that Brownlow might become a Confederate chaplain, he announced: "When I shall have made up my mind to go to hell, I will cut my throat, and go *direct,* and not travel round by way of the Southern Confederacy.[2]

In 1861, Parson Brownlow described himself: "Although I

2. E. Merton Coulter, *William G. Brownlow* (Chapel Hill: University of North Carolina Press, 1937), pp. 95, 143–144.

am now fifty-five years of age, I walk erect, have but few gray hairs, and *look* to be younger than any whiskey-drinking, to-bacco-chewing, profane-swearing Secessionist in any of the Cotton States, of forty years." [3]

During the early days of the war, he was imprisoned by Con-federate authorities. For a period, he fled Knoxville and hid out in the mountains of nearby Sevier County. He made speaking tours in the North to raise funds for the Unionists of East Ten-nessee and to re-establish his closed newspaper. The *New York Times* reported, "He is himself a legion and might safely be pit-ted against the whole Confederacy." [4] Multitudes crowded the halls where he spoke, and leading citizens contributed to his cause. By November 1863, his newspaper could reappear—now called the *Knoxville Whig and Rebel Ventilator*. He defined his sense of reconciliation: "The *mediation* we shall advocate, is that of the *cannon* and the *sword;* and our motto is—no armi-stice on land or sea, until *all* ALL the rebels, both front and rear, in arms, and in ambush are subjugated or exterminated!" [5]

It has been said that Brownlow was hated by Tennessee Con-federates the way Cromwell was hated by Ireland's Catholics. Little wonder that Brownlow biographer E. M. Coulter would conclude: "It was a strange and dangerous act to set a person of Brownlow's record to rule over a million people. In peaceful times it would have been perilous; in the confusion incident to the closing of a civil war, it might well seem preposterous." [6]

The years were full of official prosecutions and petty persecu-tion. Being the people they were, Tennesseans did not fail to react. An opponent called Brownlow and his Radicals "the party paying no taxes, riding poor horses, wearing dirty shirts, and having no use for soap." [7]

Secret societies carried out threats and counterthreats and vio-lence escalated. One creation of the times was destined to widen its influence far beyond the boundaries of the state. The Ku

3. Coulter, *William G. Brownlow*, p. 143.
4. Coulter, *William G. Brownlow*, p. 226.
5. Coulter, *William G. Brownlow*, p. 251.
6. Coulter, *William G. Brownlow*, p. 262.
7. Coulter, *William G. Brownlow*, p. 337.

Klux Klan began as a night-time diversion for a group of bored young men who gathered in an abandoned house in the town of Pulaski one December evening in 1865. As they discovered that some of their shenanigans and hooded rides over the countryside aroused more terror than amusement, the secret organization became a weapon of control. Its lawlessness in the name of order became a new factor in the state's and region's—and finally the nation's—politics.

In its early days, rhymes as well as rifles were part of the Klan's ammunition, to which Brownlow responded in kind. A Memphis newspaper carried a long poem entitled, "Death's Brigade," of which these were the opening and closing stanzas:

> The wolf is in the desert
>   And the panther in the brake.
> The fox is on his rambles
>   And the owl is wide awake;
> For now 'tis noon of darkness
>   And the world is all asleep,
> And some shall wake to glory
>   And some shall wake to weep.
>   Ku Klux.
>
> . . . . . .
>
> The misty gray is hanging
>   On the tresses of the East,
> And morn shall tell the story
>   Of the revel and the feast.
> The ghostly troop shall vanish
>   Like the light in constant cloud,
> But where they rode shall gather
>   The coffin and the shroud.
>   Ku Klux.[8]

In his Knoxville newspaper, Brownlow published a poem dedicated to himself and the state, which echoed the Klan's style:

---

8. Stanley F. Horn, *Invisible Empire: Story of the Ku Klux Klan, 1866–1871*, American History Series, No. 47 (1939; reprint edition, New York: Haskell House Publishers, Ltd., 1969), pp. 335, 336.

When midnight shrouds the sacred spot
Where traitors 'gainst their country plot,
   What man is damned the first and most,
   Damned while they tremble lest his ghost
Should haunt them with a hangman's knot,
And visions grim of gallows-post?
                    Brownlow.[9]

General Nathan Bedford Forrest, the Confederate Wizard of
the Saddle, became the Grand Wizard of the Invisible Empire in
1867. He and Dragons, Hydras, Furies, Nighthawks, and
Ghouls ruled over Realms, Dominions and Dens.

Tennessee, the last state to leave the Union, became the first
state to return to the Union. It remained a political frontier,
however. A contemporary historian observed that, throughout
1868, there was continued discord within the state. The Klan
began to spread its tentacles across other Southern states.
Within two years, Nathan Bedford Forrest resigned his membership and called for the end of the KKK. It dissolved,
reorganized, and set a pattern for generations to come, when it
would reappear during times of national and regional stress and
change.

Brownlow was kept busy fighting the Klan and numerous
other enemies, among them President Andrew Johnson. According to historian James W. Patton, the Reconstruction governor
and the tailor president "during the twenty-five years preceding
the outbreak of the Civil War, had fought each other 'system-
atically, perseveringly, and untiringly.' " [10] Failure of conviction in Johnson's impeachment trial disappointed Brownlow.
When he departed the governor's office in 1869 to go to Washington as senator, Brownlow left nine counties in Middle and
West Tennessee under martial law. Five companies occupied
the town of Pulaski, birthplace of the Klan.

In March 1875, he ended his career as senator. Two years

9. Coulter, *William G. Brownlow*, p. 336.
10. J. A. Sharp, "The Entrance of the Farmers' Alliance into Tennessee Politics,"
East Tennessee Historical Publications, No. 9, 1937.

later, he died in Knoxville. Few remained indifferent to Parson Brownlow. He was hailed as a martyred hero, a friendly and incorruptible leader who never drank, smoked, dealt a pack of cards, or saw a play at a theater. He was also denounced as a destroyer who could verbalize more vitriolic hatred than nearly any other man in American politics.

In that dual nature, Brownlow presented a magnified example of much of Tennessee's political style. Since the days of the Watauga Association and the Cumberland Compact, earliest effective attempts at self-government in America, Tennesseans seemed to know what they wanted in government and in political candidates. If their choices varied as widely as the personality and careers of the three men who went from Tennessee to the White House—Jackson and Polk and Johnson—or as sharply as machine boss Ed Crump and the populist-individualist Estes Kefauver, there were, nevertheless, several ingredients common to campaigns through the years.

These ingredients include humor, the factionalism and flair that are part of highly personal politics, and, above all, an instinct for the common mind, the instinct for success.

Invective has been the seasoning without which Tennessee politics would have lost distinctive flavor, especially in earlier days. If the preacher would save souls from damnation, and the lawyer would rescue his client from an unjust fate, the political orator would deliver his listeners from the hardships and dullness of daily life. The intensity and wit of savage verbal attack provided such diversion—and release, as well. Andrew Jackson knew this when he characterized his great opponent, Henry Clay, as "that Judas of the West." James K. Polk knew this, as he built his reputation for being one of the best stump speakers in his day: "skilled in the use of sarcasm and ridicule, and a master of the art of popular debate." Andrew Johnson knew this when he called one opposition party "a huge reptile, upon whose neck the foot of every honest man ought to be placed." [11]

11. Sharp, "The Farmers' Alliance and Tennessee Politics," p. 37.

And Boss Ed Crump knew it when he placed an advertisement in a Memphis newspaper in July 1948, describing an opposition candidate for governor:

> I have said before, and I repeat it now, that in the art galleries of Paris there are twenty-seven pictures of Judas Iscariot—none look alike but all resemble Gordon Browning; that neither his head, heart nor hand can be trusted; that he would milk his neighbor's cow through a crack in the fence; that, of two hundred and six bones in his body there isn't one that is genuine; that his heart has beaten over two billion times without a single sincere beat.[12]

Such exuberance in vilification has shocked some of the state's visitors, from time to time. When Englishman J. S. Buckingham published in 1842 his impressions of a tour of the South, he was obviously unsettled by his first-hand encounter with Tennessee politics. He wrote that he could not

> wonder at the unwillingness of men of worth and honour to enter into the stormy sea of political life, and undergo the ordeal of a popular election in this country, while they are so certain of being assailed with the most unmeasured vituperation, and made the victim of the most false and foul aspersions by their political opponents. It is shamefully bad in England . . . I thought it worse in the large cities of America; but they are both comparatively mild and fair, compared with the papers of the interior; and those of this section of Tennessee . . . are the most abusive, unjust, and unprincipled that are anywhere to be found, for, with a few honourable exceptions only, they appeared to me to sacrifice truth, honour, and courtesy, to party-feelings; hesitating at nothing to blacken the character of a political opponent, though he should be of the most pure and spotless reputation." [13]

What the itinerant observer failed to note was the number of "men of worth and honour" who did enter that stormy sea—and prevailed. He also did not realize the tradition of frontier exaggeration from which much of this verbal abuse sprang, along with its leavening companion, humor.

Tennesseans could enjoy a toast such as the one given at a

---

12. V. O. Key, Jr., *Southern Politics* (New York: Random House, 1949), p. 58.
13. J. S. Buckingham, *The Slave States of America* (London, 1842), chapter 14.

Rhea County celebration by a candidate who proclaimed himself to be "a whole-hog Democrat, to the bone, bone and all, and the marrow throw'd in!"

They could appreciate the story, preserved by journalist North Callahan, of a politician electioneering in the mountains early in the twentieth century. The candidate made the most of his military service, pointing out that he had fought the Indians, "often had no bed but the battlefield," and had "marched over the frozen ground until every step was marked with blood." Only one wizened old voter remained unimpressed. He came forward and asked,

"Did you say ye'd fit fer the Union?"

"Yes," replied the candidate.

"And agin the Indians?"

"Yes, many a time."

"And that you had slept on the ground with only the sky fer a kiver?"

"Certainly."

"And that yore feet bled in marching over the frozen ground?"

"That they did," cried the exultant candidate.

"Then I'll be danged effen ye hain't done enough fer your country," said the voter. "Go home and rest. I'll vote for the other feller." [14]

Much of the humor derived from reducing the abstract to the specific, from deflating the grandiose to the commonplace. No one used such humor more effectively than Bob Taylor, who served Tennessee in numerous political offices and could appeal to partisanship without arousing bitterness, and stir laughter without leaving pain. Campaigning in 1890, he characterized himself as a Democrat, but in such a manner as to win friends and influence people in the opposite party as well: "I am a farmer from away up the creek. I am in favor of pumpkin pie, persimmons, o'possums, hog and hominy, turnip greens, chitlins, Buchanan . . . and Democracy." [15]

14. North Callahan, *Smoky Mountain Country*, American Folkways Series (New York: Duell, Sloan and Pearce; Boston: Little, Brown & Company, 1952), p. 232.

15. Sharp, "The Farmers' Alliance and Tennessee Politics," p. 89.

Bob Taylor didn't have to go into any technical explanation of the Republican tariff he opposed after he had told his constituents that such a tariff raised the tax on wool hats and lowered it on silk ones.

Factionalism has been the raw meat, and flair (or charisma) has been the sauce for Tennessee's brand of intensely personal politics. When V. O. Key, Jr., wrote his comprehensive study, *Southern Politics,* he noted: "Tennessee's factional politics has a character all its own. The peculiar form of the coalitions and combinations that struggle for control of the state grow out of geographical diversity and the powerful influences of long-past events on the voting behavior of its citizens." [16]

East Tennessee has remained a Republican stronghold since the days of the Civil War. In the election of 1952, Sevier County, bordering the Great Smokies, could boast that, measured by percentage, it was one of the dozen best Eisenhower counties in the United States, and, out of that dozen, it led in the total majority.

Similar solidarity kept Middle and West Tennessee in the Democratic camp for most of the years from the Civil War until the Kennedy-Nixon presidential race in 1960. Ben W. Hooper, a mountain Republican prohibitionist and candidate on a fusion ticket during a period of Democratic disagreement, provided an interval of Republican governorship from 1911 to 1915. But for the most part, until the past decade, Key's assessment that Tennessee has, instead of a one-party system, *two* one-party systems, was valid. Each party staked out its area of influence, and it was alleged that Democratic Boss Crump in Memphis and Old Guard Republican leaders in East Tennessee made no serious forays into each other's spheres of command. There was suspicion that the Tennessee Republican high command contemplated victory in state races with a shudder, and that East Tennessee Democrats offered no real fight for county and district offices. Thus, for years, East Tennessee could provide the schizophrenic national contribution of liberal Democrat Estes

16. Key, *Southern Politics,* p. 59.

Kefauver in the Senate and conservative Republican national chairman Carroll Reece in the Congress.

Above all, and including all its other qualities, the nature of Tennessee politics has been personal. Comparing, in 1949, two of the nation's most firmly entrenched political machines, Key observed that, unlike Virginia, whose political machine was deeply rooted in the state's social fabric, the Tennessee organization was, at that time, a highly personal operation of Ed Crump.

To the rest of the country, he was Boss Crump, head of a big city machine that also controlled a county and state government. To Memphians, he was Mister Crump, who gave them a clean city, efficient government, and officials who did not steal from the municipality. To those who won his favor, he was cordial and obliging; those who opposed him found a willing fighter. Resisting Gordon Browning's candidacy for governor in 1948, Crump put an ad in state newspapers: "Browning, as governor for one term, converted the proud capital of Tennessee into a regular Sodom and Gomarrah, a wicked capital, reeking with sordid, vicious infamy. His handy vultures were also there. One may re-brand a hog with a smooth crop, a fork in the end of its ear, or a bit out of the bottom of its ear, yet it remains the same hog." [17] The waning effectiveness of such hyperbole was demonstrated when Browning was elected despite the Boss's denunciations.

To interview Mr. Crump could be "as difficult as trying to squeeze water out of a bale of cotton." One reporter described him just before he was first elected mayor of Memphis in 1910: "tall and rather spare for his height . . . all bone and muscle . . . a luxuriant mop of red hair." Crump followed fads in food and condensed principles into epigrams: "One of the most comfortable places to live is just inside your income"; or, "Never put a sponge on the end of a hammer if you expect to drive a nail." Just before his death in 1954, at the age of eighty, he

---

17. William D. Miller, *Mister Crump of Memphis* (Baton Rouge: Louisiana State University Press, 1964), p. 328.

could still "pass the word" and control certain elections. Those not included in "the word" could share the disappointment of the man who had hastily endorsed a candidate opposing one backed by Mr. Crump. Told that he'd been left out on a limb, "Limb, hell!," he retorted; "left out on a twig." [18]

When a young Congressman from the Third District (Chattanooga) announced in 1947 that he wanted to run for the U.S. Senate and began to campaign, without consulting the Memphis boss of more than twenty years, Crump was furious. He didn't like Estes Kefauver's independence or his ideas. During the campaign, he compared Kefauver to "a pet coon that puts its foot in your bureau drawer and when you catch him, looks the other way and hopes he will deceive any onlookers as to where his foot is and what it is into." The intent was to suggest that Kefauver's liberal record in Congress made him a "darling of the Communists." But Kefauver seized the opportunity to put on a coonskin cap, a symbol of the forthright pioneer, and declare, "I may be a pet coon but I'm not Mr. Crump's pet coon." [19]

It was all reminiscent of some of Davy Crockett's campaigns against the followers of tough old Andy Jackson. In Congress, Davy had told his constituents, "Look at my neck and you will not find any collar with a label: 'My Dog, Andrew Jackson.' " [20]

Tennesseans admired such spunkiness, even when pitted against one of their heroes. They sent Estes Kefauver to the Senate in 1948 and kept him there until his sudden death in 1963. Ironically enough, the symbol that had captured his Tennessee public led to alienation in later years among those on the national scene who dismissed the Yale Law School graduate, the stout supporter of Atlantic Union, the tough and tenacious fighter against organized crime and unchallenged monopoly, as an awkward provincial. The common people across the United

18. Miller, *Mr. Crump*, pp. 73, 74.

19. Callahan, *Smoky Mountain Country*, p. 236.

20. David Crockett, *A Narrative of the Life of David Crockett of the State of Tennessee*, facsimile edition with annotations and an introduction by James A. Shackford and Stanley J. Folmsbee (Knoxville: University of Tennessee Press, 1973), p. 211.

States responded to him, but organization men perceived the danger to themselves of his old frontier independence amidst the cool expediences of the New Frontier accommodation. For witty newsmen and sophisticated analysts, it seemed easier to ridicule Kefauver than to comprehend him; he was perhaps the most paradoxical of any public figure in Tennessee's public life. But one thing he remained throughout his career: the personal politician. The political analyst-historian, Theodore H. White, assessed Kefauver's magic as the ability to convince almost anyone—farmer, blue-collar worker, or housewife—that politics is that person himself. Out of his own zest and enjoyment for politics, Kefauver communicated the idea that politics is fun; that the individual can take part in it, and that a candidate needs the individual.

If he shook 25,000 hands across the state in one senatorial race, Kefauver simply raised his effort to a higher degree in his race across America for the presidential nomination in 1952 and 1956. The *New York Times* spoke of his crime-and-politics exposures as the cardinal sin for which the big city machines were not likely to forgive him; they were also the source of his strength. "To many Americans, sick of the corruption they hear about so often . . . Mr. Kefauver stands as a courageous fighter for clean government." [21]

A large, soft-spoken, slightly remote man, despite his easygoing friendliness, Kefauver was a reminder of those first Tennesseans who knew how they wanted their government to function and were willing to work, grubbily as well as grandly, to make it so. It was not accidental that a key provision in their first compact of self-government had made possible the recall of corrupt officials.

No record of the political phenomenon of Tennessee would be complete, however, without the War of the Roses and Bob and Alf Taylor. During the troubled days of 1886, when bile and gall spewed from the Civil War had left an embittered government and electorate, two brothers from Happy Valley in

21. Joseph B. Gorman, *Kefauver: A Political Biography* (New York: Oxford University Press, 1971), p. 230.

northeastern Carter County became good-natured opponents for the governor's office. They brought zeal tempered by laughter to relieve the tension and hate surrounding a generally abrasive partisan politics.

The Taylors were a solid, well-connected family—the father a Whig, educated at Washington College in Tennessee and at Princeton, the mother a member of the prominent Democratic family of Haynes—whose two most famous sons dramatized the family's and the state's divisions, yet managed to heal rather than aggravate old wounds.

Robert L. was a Democrat, Alfred A., a Republican; when it was observed that despite their different parties they were "two roses from the same garden," their contest was named the War of the Roses. Bob claimed the white rose of York and Alf the red rose of Lancaster as they stumped the state. During joint debates, they played the fiddle—not too well—honed their wit—not too savagely—and directed their fulsome oratory to issues of the day—not too exhaustively.

Those issues were grim enough: a heavy public debt, regulation of railroads, prison reform, inadequate public education; and a burdened public welcomed the diversion of brothers whose good humor was as refreshing as mountain spring-water. As historian Daniel M. Robison has said,

> They appeared at a time when the state's economic and social structure had undergone a violent change. Their solution had left the public with a case of frayed nerves. On the horizon appeared signs of future storms . . . The War of the Roses was a happy interlude . . . Nothing does more good for frayed nerves than genuine, hearty laughter, and this "Bob" and "Alf" provided for the people of Tennessee . . . One has the feeling that a rural editor voiced the sentiment of Tennessee when he asked, "Why not have a little fun as we go along?" [22]

The Taylors understood that political gatherings were for entertainment as well as enlightenment. They had put in some practice along this line by once writing a play. The comedy

22. Daniel M. Robison, *Bob Taylor and the Agrarian Revolt in Tennessee* (Chapel Hill: University of North Carolina Press, 1935), p. 69.

"raised enough money to carpet a lot of Methodist churches in the region," and, according to one chronicler, contained a scene which demonstrated the Taylors' understanding of several facts of their fellow Tennesseans' character. A mountain man is asked to testify about a murder on Hell Creek but says he doesn't know much about it.

"Then tell what you know."

"All I know is this," drawls the witness.

"We was all up thar at the big dance celebratin' Robert E. Lee's birthday. The fiddles was playin' and we was swingin' corners, and the boys got to slappin' each other on the back as they swung. Finally one of them slapped too hard and the other knocked him down. His brother shot that feller, and that feller's brother cut t'other feller's throat, and the feller that was knocked down drawed his knife and cut that feller's liver out; the old man of the house got mad and run to the bed, turned up the tick and grabbed his shotgun and turned both barrels loose on the crowd, and I saw there was goin' to be trouble and I left." [23]

The Taylors could discuss the troubles facing their state, but leave their listeners less troubled afterward. They reveled in dramatizing their differences and their beliefs. Once, responding to Republican criticism of his use of the fiddle, and seeking to underscore the influence of Radical Republicans among his opposition, Bob simply mounted the rostrum and laid his fiddle on the speaker's table, then placed beside it a carpetbag brought for the occasion. Addressing the audience, he asked it to choose between the fiddle and the carpetbag. This may have been oversimplification of the highest order, but it was good politicking.

Those who had "dreaded an unseemly or disgusting wrangle between two brothers" [24] had their fears quieted after the first of forty-one debates that took them across the state. They traveled together, ate together, awaited late trains together, spoke to throngs that "were never at any point in the smallest counties less than six thousand people; at Memphis there were fifteen thousand people; at Jackson, ten thousand; at Nashville, twenty-

23. Callahan, *Smoky Mountain Country,* p. 59.

24. James P. Taylor et al., *Life and Career of Robert Love Taylor,* p. 165.

five thousand.'' But while each berated and deplored the other's politics, neither lost his temper or his humor.

Bob summed up their relationship at the close of one memorable speech: ''Let me assure you that I today love the man who has borne the Republican banner as dearly as when, in the good old days long ago, we slept side by side in the trundle-bed and shared our youthful joys and griefs. I have never seen the hour when I would not willingly lay down my life to save him, nor have I seen the dawn of the day when I would lay down my life to destroy his party.'' [25]

Thus they criss-crossed Tennessee and captured the nation's attention: stealing each other's speeches, playing pranks and jokes, fiddling, declaiming from stump and rostrum, all to the tune of Alf's ''Yankee Doodle'' and Bob's ''Dixie.'' (In later years, they would join the lyceum circuit and entertain sellout audiences across the nation, from New York to the Northwest, with their joint speech entitled ''Yankee Doodle and Dixie.'')

When it was learned that a debate in Memphis was scheduled for the same day that Mr. Barnum's circus would be performing, there was speculation about which event would attract the larger audience. One editor was relieved when the gubernatorial candidates changed their date so that Barnum might get a crowd.

When the votes were finally cast on election day, Bob won by a majority of 13,000. It was an unprecedented Democratic lead. And even though defeated, Alf had also set a record—the largest Republican vote in Tennessee until that date. Each of them went on to serve Tennessee for many years: Bob as governor for three terms, and as congressman and senator; Alf, as governor once and three times as a congressman. The most significant single result of the War of the Roses had been Bob's achievement in consolidating his party, which had been threatened with overthrow and collapse by its factional bitterness. He would remain a conciliator throughout his career.

If the Taylors ''did not burden the minds of their hearers unduly,'' as one editor lamented, they did remind contemporary

25. James P. Taylor et al., *Life and Career of Robert Love Taylor*, p. 160.

and future Tennesseans of the accuracy of "Rule Number Five," an unwritten law that the state's politicians overlooked to their regret; according to tradition, it decreed: "Don't take yourself too damned seriously."

From the days of the Sevier-Tipton feud through the 1908 slaying of editor and ex-senator Edward Ward Carmack on the streets of Nashville by a political opponent, to the post-World War II revolt in McMinn County, when ex-GIs laid siege to local entrenched authorities and forced them to flee the county, political life in Tennessee has been characterized by strife—and accommodation; strong personalities—and deep sensitivity to the importance of democracy at its grass roots. The accommodation could lead to such fence-straddling as that of a reputed candidate who did not wish to confront the issue of a tax increase too definitely: "Folks," he said, "there's two things I want to promise about taxes: if they're too high, we'll lower 'em; if they're too low, we'll hist 'em."

When winning personalities emerged, they were kept mindful of the fact that their power came from the people. The judgment of one of Andrew Jackson's old neighbors was more than a mere comment on popularity when he called the president a prince of hospitality, not because he entertained many people but because a peddler was as welcome at the Hermitage as the president of the United States.

In recent times, when Albert Gore—who had served in the U.S. Congress and Senate—lost the senate race of 1970 to Chattanooga congressman and candy manufacturing heir William Brock, there were many surprised observers around the country. They had not expected the defeat of the man who overcame in 1952 the mighty Kenneth McKellar and his Crump support and then went on to become a combination of populist-intellectual at the national level. Perhaps the critical factor in Gore's defeat was stated best by a thoughtful reporter who discussed many major and minor causes and then observed that the Senator had remembered the challenge to be a statesman but forgotten the necessity to be a politician.

At its best, Tennessee has contributed both statesmen and politicians to the nation. No other area of its daily and public life has demonstrated more consistently than its politics the truth that Tennessee is divided in its unity and unified in its diversity. In its politics, Tennessee retained the frontier image into the mid-twentieth century. In grim times, it has sometimes re- minded Americans that Rule Number Five is still in effect—and still a bracing tonic.

7

Dreamers and Doers

IN the season after wheat was harvested, before corn was ripe, when crops were "laid by," through the long drowsy days of late summer, while insects droned in meadows at midday and distant stars seemed near as fireflies in the warm velvety evenings, during the opening decades of the nineteenth century, Tennesseans gathered in great, informal congregations to exhort and listen and experience religion at a phenomenon known as the camp meeting.

It was a kind of assembly unique to the frontier, and it began, flourished, and gradually waned in the Old Southwest of Kentucky and Tennessee especially. Its development might seem inevitable, given the facts of Tennessee's frontier—long distances separating homesteads and communities, raw wilderness demanding harsh daily toil, loneliness born of geography and isolation—combined with the historic background of recent release from a stratified class society. There was also the more intangible but no less intense factor of responsibility, sometimes anxiety, among those cut off by the Reformation from the mediation of any priesthood. With no intercessor between individual and God, each person bore responsibility for his own human conscience and her own search for divine grace.

This was a responsibility not lightly assumed. But the vast majority of early Tennesseans believed that paradise was attainable, certainly in the next world and—possibly—in this one.

Their belief led to two distinctive and sometimes conflicting movements. By far the largest and most enduring involved a revealed religion, born of faith, inspiring people to look to personal salvation and a heaven after death. The other, sporadic and experimental, involved earthly utopias, the result of reason and good works, inviting people to live in the reality of a community brotherhood as one example of a haven before death. Faith and works, hope for the hereafter, and models for the present—knowledge of each is essential to an understanding of Tennessee.

The camp meeting was a colorful manifestation of the people's creeds, character, hungers, and style. Here, again, they were typically independent, suspicious of any "official" religion, having rejected from the very beginning in their search for freedom the Church of England in both the Old World and the New. A paid ministry and an organized church did not seem to them essential to an individual's faith or morality.

When the first draft of Tennessee's constitution was presented, there was an interesting difference between it and the North Carolina constitution, which had served as its model. Historian T. P. Abernethy has described that difference and the response it received:

> The provision of the North Carolina instrument requiring office-holders to believe in God, a future state of rewards and punishments, and the divine authority of the Old and New Testaments, was omitted. A motion was made from the floor to restore this provision and the proposal was accepted. The liberals were able to do no more than secure the elision of the last clause of this Presbyterian profession of faith. Andrew Jackson took a leading part in fighting this stand of the dogmatists, and on his side were most of the prominent men of the convention. The spirit of the French Revolution was struggling on the frontier with the spirit of John Calvin, and the future leader of American Democracy here made his debut as a liberal.[1]

It is also interesting to note that George Sevier, son of the man who embodied so much of the spirit of early Tennessee,

---

1. T. P. Abernethy, *From Frontier to Plantation in Tennessee* (Chapel Hill: University of North Carolina Press, 1932), p. 136.

wrote of his father, John, that he "never made a profession of religion—in his younger days he seems to have been more attached to the Baptist church (to whom he gave three acres of land to build a church in the town of New Market, Rockingham County, Virginia)." [2]

Religion was deeply personal and highly informal. Congregations gathered as a result of individual needs and efforts; church structures came later.

Presbyterians had arrived earliest, part of the Scotch-Irish influence in the Watauga and Holston settlements, where the Rev. Charles Cummings preached in 1777. But the Baptist Tidence Lane came in 1778 or '79, and Methodist Jeremiah Lambert only a short while later. The three denominations that would dominate the state's religious life had planted their seed.

Without buildings or a regular ministry, people assembled for services in homes; then came larger services, sometimes called "protracted meetings." It was on one of these occasions that the event known as a camp meeting was born.

According to John McGee, a Methodist minister of Sumner County, Tennessee, he and his brother William, who was a Presbyterian minister, joined James McGready, also a Presbyterian, in holding a "sacramental solemnity" at his church at Red River, Kentucky, in 1799. At the end of the meeting, a woman in the congregation began to shout. John McGee remained behind after other clergymen had withdrawn and "went among the congregation exhorting. The shouting became general and many souls were saved." [3]

At this same Red River gathering, a family who did not have enough horses for each member to ride to the church simply stocked a wagon with provisions and camped on the grounds while the meeting was in progress.

Born of common sense and improvisation, such encampments grew and became both cause and result of the so-called Great Awakening of the early nineteenth century. From distances as far as forty, fifty, and more miles, they came in wagons, car-

2. Carl S. Driver, *John Sevier* (Chapel Hill: University of North Carolina Press, 1932), pp. 213–214.

3. Abernethy, *Frontier to Plantation*, pp. 212–213.

riages, a wide array of vehicles, and raised their tents—of cotton sailcloth, muslin, old quilts hung over poles, or of more sturdy sticks and logs, or brush arbors—ranged along improvised rows and "streets." To accommodate the needs of these throngs, the camp site had to be near springs or a river for the water supply, with pasture available for the horses and firewood for the cooking.

Focal point of the sprawling scene was the pulpit, usually a platform raised high enough above the audience so that a succession of preachers could command the listeners' attention despite a constant swirl of distractions. Seats were most often rows of logs smoothed along one side; men and women were segregated—women to the right and men to the left of the pulpit. Negroes were separated into the area behind the pulpit but their service often became indistinguishable from that of the white participants as shouting, singing, and other excitement mounted and melted together in one ecstatic hullabaloo.

They spent the summer days and nights surrounded by seemingly endless expanses of green virgin forest, supplied with a bounty of cold pure water, breathing the acrid blue wood-smoke from rows of campfires and the rich smells of food cooking over glowing red coals, listening to the greetings of old friends, the voices of children playing, crying, growing drowsy, the stamping of the horses, and the bedlam of the meeting itself once the services had begun.

Lorenzo Dow, the gloomy Methodist, might once have described Tennessee as "a Sink of Iniquity, a Black Pit of Irreligion," but these participants did not share his opinion. One Presbyterian wrote in 1840 of the response to revival time:

> The laborer quitted his task; Age snatched his crutch; Youth forgot his pastime; the plow was left in the furrow; the deer enjoyed a respite upon the mountains; business of all kinds was suspended; dwelling houses were deserted; whole neighborhoods were emptied; bold hunters and sober matrons, young women and maidens, and little children, flocked to the common center of attraction; every difficulty was surmounted, every risk ventured to be present at the camp-meeting.[4]

4. Charles A. Johnson, *The Frontier Camp Meeting* (Dallas: Southern Methodist University Press, 1955), p. 51.

Many of the revivals involved only a few hundred participants; the more famous ones drew thousands, such as those in
north-central Tennessee, which were ignited by that landmark of
all American camp meetings, the one at Cane Ridge, Kentucky,
in August 1801. Here, at a kind of early-day Woodstock, between ten and twenty-five thousand (the estimates vary wildly)
gathered for six days of worship and hysteria, devotion and
frenzy, individual and communal experience.

It was this combination of faith and fervor, spiritual exalta-
tion and physical exertion that distinguished the camp meeting.
Throughout each day of the meeting, interspersed with hymn-
singing, sermons were delivered, one after the other, always
with a central thought "to show sinners where they stand, and
where they might land."

By the time evening arrived, with candles and campfires
flickering in the midst of the vast brooding darkness and the
exhortations growing more impassioned, emotions had reached
a feverish pitch. While some of the affected "fell down like
slain men in battle," others were seized by all manner of con-
tortions. These were known as "exercises": the falling, dancing, rolling, laughing, singing, jerking, or barking exercise.
Falling was "common among all classes, from the philosopher
to the clown." [5] The most unusual exercises were the latter
two. Jerking might involve only the head snapping back and
forth or side to side, sometimes with such force that bonnets and
caps would fly or long hair "crack almost as loud as a
wagoner's whip"; or it might engage the entire body in long
spasmodic vibrations. The barking exercise seems to have origi-
nated in East Tennessee, when an afflicted jerker clutched a tree
for support. Eventually, small groups of revivalists would be
found gathered around a tree, yelping and barking, "treeing the
devil."

The "natural" religion of the frontier individualist, such as
Boone and Sevier, was swept aside by the "revealed" religion
of the frontier evangelist and the community revival. There
were those who rejoiced and those who were dismayed by the
development. A contemporary judge voiced his approval:

5. J. T. Moore and Austin Foster, *Tennessee,* p. 334.

I have always been in favor of camp meetings . . . It is a storm, it purifies the atmosphere. It moves upon the waters and harrows up the deep; in its course it fells the most stubborn oak; it is a religious enthusiasm that throttles sin and purifies the soul . . . I have seen at one of those camp meetings the forked lightning playing over the largest assemblages and the wild thunder leaping from head to head, and have seen a hundred women with the jerks, the result of religious enthusiasm.[6]

Among those not fully in harmony with an enthusiasm that often seemed excessive, and the attendant extracurricular activities that could result in secular romance more than repentance at the mourner's bench, were some of the Presbyterians who had been early innovators of the camp meetings. As historian Charles A. Johnson has pointed out, "at the same time that the Presbyterians were discontinuing the camp meeting, the Methodists were beginning to take it to their hearts as their own." Throughout their most prolific years, "camp meetings were carried on by a great number of denominations, large and small," but "by 1825 the camp meeting was almost exclusively a Methodist institution." [7]

For some fifty years, from 1800 to mid-century, the camp meeting was a colorful, powerful influence in all parts of Tennessee. But even as it waxed and waned, quieter ministers and earnest followers were establishing the various churches that would become central to Tennessee's formal religious life. Other denominations were joining the Big Three.

Dividing from earlier conservative Protestant congregations, early in the 1800s the Church of Christ began a growth that would result in the state's fourth largest membership. By 1827, a Protestant Episcopal Church was established in Franklin by the Rev. James H. Otey. Lutherans in Sullivan County had organized a church in the late 1700s, but their Synod of Tennessee was not created until 1820. Priests of the Roman Catholic faith visited Tennessee in its earliest years of discovery and settlement, but it was not until 1830 that a parish was formed, a

6. J. T. Moore and Austin Foster, *Tennessee*, p. 332.
7. C. A. Johnson, *Frontier Camp Meeting*, p. 80.

church erected—in Nashville. A Hebrew congregation was established in Memphis in 1852, and one in Nashville the following year. As early as 1796, Quakers from North Carolina and Virginia settled in Tennessee, but their town of Friendsville was not laid out until 1852. They opposed both slavery and war, and, during the Civil War, they were caught in a cruel dilemma.

The year after the war, black congregations began to organize their own churches. During slavery, servants had often attended church with their owners, sitting in separate pews or sections. But testimony gathered in the 1930s by the Federal Writers' Project, from some former Tennessee slaves and recently published by Lowell H. Harrison, suggests that religious gatherings among the slaves were not encouraged so much as has been generally believed. Ann Matthews, in Middle Tennessee, remembered: "During slavery the white folks didn't want the Negroes to sing and pray, but they would turn a pot down and meet at the pot in the night and sing and pray and the white folks wouldn't hear them." [8]

The custom of leaving this unusual signal was mentioned by another ex-slave: "The white folks wouldn't let the slaves have a book or paper for fear they'd learn something, and if they wanted to pray they'd turn a kettle down at their cabin door." [9]

When emancipation abolished the need for subterfuge, Negro churches multiplied rapidly.

Differences were commonplace among and within these various congregations. Some of the differences would bear influence through the years. Sometimes the conflicts were solved by the old familiar method of secession. When the Cumberland Presbytery of Middle Tennessee was severely criticized for its participation in the revival movement and what seemed a subsequent relaxation of educational standards for its ministers, the congregation divided from its parent and formed the Cumberland Presbyterian Church in 1810. Within four decades, the offspring was larger than the main body of Tennessee Presbyterians.

8. Lowell H. Harrison, "Recollections of Some Tennessee Slaves," *Tennessee Historical Quarterly*, XXXIII, no. 2 (Summer 1974), p. 185.

9. Harrison, "Recollections of Tennessee Slaves," p. 185.

As national and regional debate over slavery and abolition intensified, arguments in the churches on this issue also increased. In 1845, the Methodist Episcopal Church, South, was formed, after the General Conference of the full congregation had condemned slavery. The Southern Methodists, as they were informally known, established their headquarters and independent publishing firm in Nashville.

During the same year and for the same basic reason, a Southern Baptist Church was established. It would soon become the largest denomination in Tennessee and one of the largest in the nation, and it would continue as Southern Baptist until the present day.

Of all the denominations, Baptists were most given to fission, to dividing into separate entities. Some of the spirit and the hazard surrounding this separatism was described by one of the old-time leaders, Dr. J. J. Burnett:

> They, and their sires, had fought for civil and religious liberty, for the rights of the individual, the rights of the common people, and of the local church. They had thus either contracted or inherited a religious bias in the direction of individualism and local church independence, or Baptist democracy . . . Good men actually feared centralization, and the people in general had no taste for an aristocracy of any kind, ministerial or otherwise . . . Neither had they learned by experience or observation the wisdom and necessity of co-operation in order to [achieve] largest service and greatest results in the Lord's work.[10]

In 1835, there were these various orders officially listed in the denomination's publication, *Baptist:* United, Separate, Regular, Particular, and General Baptists.

One chief cause of division among Baptists concerned sending missionaries to foreign countries and sometimes to other areas in this country. One church recorded in its minutes of 1839 that "on further consideration furrin missions were protested against," and in 1848 another congregation charged a neighboring church with "Being too friendly with the mishean-

---

10. J. J. Burnett, *Sketches of Tennessee's Pioneer Baptist Preachers* (Nashville: Marshall and Bruce, 1919), p. 15.

ary Baptists.'' [11] These entries reflect another attitude characteristic of many early Baptists: their suspicion of education.

This suspicion was in special contrast to the Presbyterians, who insisted upon an educated ministry and encouraged an educated public. Perhaps it was another demonstration of Baptist democracy and unyielding individualism that led them to cherish revelation more than education, and heed a "call" to preach that could allow a man to be behind the plow on Saturday and in the pulpit for the first time on Sunday. One historian of the frontier has spoken of "the rising Baptists, who were rather indifferent to learning but as adamant about the separation of church and state as about immersion.'' [12]

Eventually those associations that rejected missions assumed the title of Primitive or Hard-Shell Baptists. Conceived in controversy, they bore other groups that also went their own way: Secret Order, Hard Side, Progressive, and Two-Seeder Baptists. The latter group, Two-Seed-in-the-Spirit believers, held the doctrine that a person was born "eternally damned or eternally justified.'' Such hints of predestination seemed to most Baptists closer to Presbyterian beliefs than to their own.

Church divisions usually reflected another Tennessee characteristic: they were highly personal. No issue remained merely intellectual or doctrinal for long. When a church in Powell Valley, for instance, was torn by controversy early in the 1900s, members chose either the Big John Miller Side or the Manny Weaver Side.

Theodore Roosevelt, describing the *Winning Of the West,* evaluated both the strengths and weaknesses of the frontier camp meetings and found them, on the whole, a gain for moral responsibility. His judgment of the preachers, especially the long-suffering circuit riders, was even more affirmative: despite their narrowness and occasional vanity, these men were earnest, persevering and self-sacrificing to the point of heroism. Sick-

11. L. Edwards, "Primitive Baptists" (M.A. thesis, University of Tennessee, 1941), p. 37.

12. Arthur K. Moore, *The Frontier Mind: A Cultural Analysis of the Kentucky Frontiersman* (Lexington: University Press of Kentucky, 1957), p. 226.

ness, flood, storm, and hostility from early red men and later white savages, took a toll among them.

One of the best known, the man who introduced the circuit system to Tennessee, was Bishop Francis Asbury, "the prophet and shepherd of the long road." He fulfilled Charles Johnson's statement that "the saddlebag preacher often outworked the farmer, outrode the hunter, and outdistanced the fur trader."

In May 1788, at the Nelson house in the vicinity of the present Johnson City, Bishop Asbury preached his first sermon in what is now Tennessee. In September 1815, he held his last conference at Bethlehem Church, some three miles from the present town of Lebanon. During those intervening twenty-seven years, he made some twenty trips into Tennessee, laboring up and down "the mighty Alps" of its mountains, enduring all conditions of weather outdoors and housekeeping indoors, preaching salvation and "order, order, good order." He found the "kindest souls in the world," and he also found bedbugs and fleas—or they found him.

He lamented, "But kindness will not make a crowded log cabin, twelve feet by ten, agreeable: without are cold and rain; and within, six adults and as many children, one of which is all motion; the dogs too, must sometimes be admitted." [13]

Riding a sparsely settled wilderness country in all weathers, assured of pay so meager that he could "hardly command my own coat on my yearly allowance," suffering chills and fevers so intense that he sometimes had to be lifted into his saddle and tied on for the journey, Asbury came to understand the men and women among whom he labored. He observed in their daily lives a tension that would remain through generations to follow: between solid land and intangible spirit, between accumulated property and uplifted souls.

There was further division here: between those who believed paradise was possible only in another world, and those who worked to bring conditions to greater perfectibility here on this earth. While churches were being founded, and revealed re-

13. C. A. Johnson, *Frontier Camp Meeting*, pp. 81, 156.

ligion was capturing converts across Tennessee, there were also continuous dreams and scattered groups seeking to establish an ideal human community somewhere in the state. Hope of heaven and dream of utopia coexisted, sometimes harmoniously, sometimes grudgingly.

Since that hot summer of 1540 when Hernando de Soto prowled the Cherokee and Chickasaw country seeking for the fabled province called Chisca, rich in gold and copper, there had been all sorts of optimists seeking instant happiness and fortune in the Tennessee country.

There was the learned and orderly German, Christian Priber, who arrived among the Overhill Cherokees in 1736 with his strongbox of books, papers, ink, and plans for "Paradise," a republic in which all lodgings, goods, and children would be under the equal ownership of all and each person would work for the common good. For the Western border, a Philadelphia merchant named Samuel Hazard made plans as early as 1755 to petition the King for a charter that would allow the erection of a "Separate Government" in the country that is now West Tennessee. His scheme embraced a vast area of land, and its outstanding feature was freedom of worship—for Protestants. Hazard claimed between four and five thousand subscribers before his sudden death in England while he was arranging a return to the New World and support for his petition. A later proposition for a colony to be called "Georgiana," after the King, was published in 1772. This was to be a fair and fruitful country incorporating West Tennessee, North Mississippi, and West Kentucky. It, too, came to naught.

These early projects for West Tennessee, including a state named "Chickasawria," were chiefly colonization schemes, but several later proposals were results of the old Tennessee penchant for secession. Between 1830 and 1832, the Western District vented its resentment at what seemed to be discrimination in internal improvements and educational institutions by contemplating separation from the sections which are now Middle and East Tennessee. This new commonwealth was to be called Jackson, or Memphis, or Chickasaw, depending perhaps on whether the settlers' mood at the time was for local heroes, grandiose antiquities, or native neighbors. Before a name became necessary, the movement had faded into oblivion.

The settlements that sprang up in response to the search for a more harmonious community life are more significant, however. Dreams of them began as early as 1748, when the peripatetic Sir Alexander Cuming proposed to the British ministry that he should help deliver and restore the Jewish people to a new homeland, located in the Cherokee country of America. He gained attention of some learned Jewish leaders, but none of the 300,000 Jewish families he offered to settle "in the Cherokee Mountains" ever materialized.

Moses Fisk's attempts to lay out a planned town did materialize—at Hilham, in the present Overton County, in 1805. A native of Massachusetts and a graduate of Dartmouth College, Fisk came to Tennessee to found a mission for the Cherokees. This was never realized, but a Fisk Female Academy, the first institution of its kind in the South, was established at Hilham. Large sums of money were invested in planning and developing the town, but never succeeded in creating the model metropolis Fisk hoped for.

Gruetli, on the Cumberland Plateau, came into being in 1870, not so much as an ideal of goodness as a dream among some German Swiss of the good life in a new land. The fulsome promotional literature they read in Switzerland, however, was not matched by the hard reality they found on land that required a seven-day week of back-breaking labor if they were to prosper. Many of the fewer than one hundred who finally arrived on the Plateau soon left to find work elsewhere. A few remained, but Gruetli never became the counterpart of Switzerland—with fertility—that had been depicted.

In a more idealistic vein, an Indiana newspaperman, Charles A. Wayland, established the Ruskin Colony in Dickson County in 1894. Wayland has been described as "the greatest propagandist of Socialism that has ever lived." [14] His desire, fostered by the writings of John Ruskin, was to create "an agrarian paradise

14. Folmsbee, Corlew, and Mitchell, *Tennessee,* p. 427.

far from the noise and strife of the complex industrial society."
A sawmill, grist mill, bakery, blacksmith shop, and similar essential services were established, along with a chewing-gum factory and a manufacturing plant for leather suspenders. An institution called the College of New Economy was opened. But eventually the isolated community proved to be too far from the complex industrial society it shunned. Political and philosophical differences forced rifts between individuals. Financial failure sealed its doom in 1901.

But it was Nashoba in West Tennessee and Rugby in East Tennessee that represented a special utopian idealism as counterpoint to religious denominationalism expressing much of the state's spiritual life. Each was relatively small, short-lived, and experimental. Each failed. But the experiments involved unusual and imaginative personalities, and the failures represented response to flagrant injustices of the times.

"Ask *why!*" Frances Wright said. She was one of those who find it necessary to question, rather than to believe, to change, rather than to accept.

A wealthy Scotswoman, tall, thin, and extremely pretty, according to contemporaries, Frances Wright held advanced ideas on marriage and religion and politics. She shared these ideas with immense audiences in Europe and America, where her grace and eloquence assumed almost legendary proportions. In 1818, when she and her sister first visited America, she fell in love with the fresh, vital young country—as she did with the charming and aging hero, Lafayette, soon after she returned to Europe. The two came to the United States together in 1824, and on this trip, Frances Wright traveled to the South and saw slavery firsthand. She talked about it with Thomas Jefferson, considered its effects on whites as well as blacks, pondered the helpless, hopeless condition of some one and a half million slaves. She decided that they must be educated for an eventual freedom she was sure would come, and they must be prepared to earn their own livelihood, develop their own talents. Whites must be inspired to consider that time and hasten its arrival.

Therefore, in October 1825, negotiating with representatives of Andrew Jackson, Frances Wright purchased 1,940 acres on both sides of the Wolf River some dozen miles northeast of Memphis. She called her plantation "Nashoba," Chickasaw for "wolf," and settled it with a small group of slaves she had purchased who were to be educated and trained to become their own masters. Land was cleared—but much of it was discovered to be of poor quality. Crops were planted the following spring, but the weather turned erratic. Before harvest time, malaria, swamp fever, and other illness had sent Frances Wright back to the British Isles.

When she returned, some months later, she worked in the fields, sought opinion to support her venture, invested more and more of her fortune in a dream that was turning into a nightmare. She could not overcome the combination of poor management, apparently indifferent farm effort, and the suspicion and hostility of neighbors, who had denounced her community as a center of free love and miscegenation.

In 1830, Frances Wright took the blacks who had lived at Nashoba to Haiti, where she had made arrangements with the president for them to settle and begin a new life in his country. The colony that had appeared so desolate in reality to Mrs. Trollope and other visiting Europeans, and so exciting in purpose and potential to its founder, was no more.

But in her *Explanatory Notes on Nashoba*, Frances Wright had delineated her ambition: "To develop all the intellectual and physical powers of all human beings, without regard to sex or condition, class, race, nation or color." [15] It was a vision as timely then as now.

Rugby, founded about 1880 by English author Thomas Hughes with royalties from his successful novel, *Tom Brown's School Days*, was designed to provide a haven for the younger sons of English gentry. Barred by the laws of primogeniture from inheriting family estates or titles, they suffered an especially debilitating discrimination. Reared to live as aristocrats, they were denied in adolescence the preparation and in adulthood the legitimate means to maintain their gentility or earn a

---

15. Richard Stiller, *Commune on the Frontier: The Story of Frances Wright*, Women of America Series (New York: Thomas Y. Crowell, 1972), p. 245.

livelihood. Hughes wished to open a new world to some of these second and third and fourth sons.

In Tennessee's Scott, Morgan, and Fentress counties, Hughes purchased more than 75,000 acres. He would establish here a society based on culture and co-operation. Its excellence would be achieved through competition, but it would be a competition of who could raise the best crops "or write the best books or articles; teach best, govern best; in a word, live most nobly,— surely here may well be scope enough for all energy, without the rivalry of shop-keeping, and the tricks of trade,—the adulteration, puffing and feverish meannesses which follow too surely in its train." [16]

Hughes also hoped that "a good stream of Englishmen into the Southern states" might help heal some of the wounds that still remained in the region as an aftermath of the Civil War.

An English village was created in the rugged Cumberland Mountains. There was a library of some 7,000 volumes, an Episcopalian church with rosewood organ from England, a well-financed school and well-appointed inn, and numerous residences and business establishments. Graveled walks led to swimming areas and to tennis courts in the woods. Some 400 residents enjoyed a social club, literary and dramatic presentations, and an agricultural and horticultural society.

Despite all this construction, there were forces working against the colony's success. Rugby historian Brian Stagg has summed up some of them: "Litigation over land titles, absentee corporation rule, and the difficulties of adaptation to a foreign clime . . . Late in 1881 a typhoid epidemic struck that killed seven of the colonists. The already publicized colony soon found itself famous for its supposed 'unhealthfulness.' " [17]

There was another factor in Rugby's failure that cannot be discounted. Gilbert Govan and James Livingood describe it well in their history, *The Chattanooga Country:*

16. Govan and Livingood, *Chattanooga Country*, p. 342.

17. Brian L. Stagg, "Tennessee's Rugby Colony," in *More Landmarks of Tennessee History,* edited by Robert M. McBride (Nashville: Tennessee History Society, Tennessee Historical Commission, 1969), p. 279.

A great gulf existed between the natives and the settlers, who held themselves aloof from the mountain people. The colonists persistently clung to the manners and speech of the homeland, which caused their new neighbors to think of them as peculiar. One amusing story illustrates a part of this difference. An old man of the neighborhood died and as there was no native preacher to hold the service, the rector at Rugby was called on. "After reading the Episcopal burial service," a contemporary account reads, "upon which the mountaineers looked with suspicion as being the 'quare doin's' of those 'furriners,' the rector solemnly announced, 'And now will all the friends of the deceased please pass around the bier?' The elder son could stand this blasphemy no longer and he jumped to his feet and shouted, 'I know Pa was a drinkin' man, but I'll be danged if yer serve drinks at his funeral.' " [18]

The lack of communication and understanding between natives and newcomers has also been described by Esther Sharp Sanderson, in her *County Scott and Its Mountain Folk:*

> In the beautiful, old English-type homes aristocracy held sway, much to the amazement of the rural pioneers, who had different ideas of life in the wilds of East Tennessee. The latter soon learned that these young "aristocrats of the cloth" had no more use for a bull-tongue plow than a razor-backed hog had for a side-saddle . . . Those natives knew that it took "guts, grit and gizzard" to make a go of farming in this region.[19]

Thomas Hughes left Rugby in 1887, never to return.

Guts, grit, and gizzard—these had been part of the old camp meetings, along with repentance and salvation. Tennessee revivals or Tennessee Utopias, they had in common a basic faith: the individual was of central importance, and progress— whether the soul's salvation or the community's improvement—was possible, indeed probable.

Tennesseans moved their meetings indoors; as their way of life grew gradually less rural, more urban, their churches tended to become larger, more separate. But even as they clustered in

18. Govan and Livingood, *Chattanooga Country,* p. 342.
19. Esther Sharp Sanderson, *County Scott and Its Mountain Folk* (Huntsville: privately published, 1958), p. 79.

cities and gathered in more formal congregations, the people retained much of the shrewd innocence, the frontier optimism running like a strong underground current beneath the surface trappings of a sophisticated twentieth-century world of technology and depersonalization.

Statistics suggest the nature of Tennessee's more recent religious affiliations. From the turn of the century until 1936, Baptists remained the largest and grew faster than any other denomination. In 1936, they could claim more than 43 percent of the total church membership of the state. Methodists were 28 percent; the Presbyterians, whose influence was so early and so strong, held only 8 percent of Tennessee's church members.[20] By 1971, the Southern Baptists, almost a million strong, along with their smaller independent relatives, the Freewill Baptists and the Missionary Baptists, had held their numerical dominance. United Methodists and the Presbyterian Church U.S.A. and Cumberland Presbytery followed in second and third order. The Churches of Christ, along with the Disciples of Christ and the Christian Church, were increasing in size and influence; the Episcopalians and Church of God congregations ranked fifth and sixth in numbers of members.[21] The strong religious image of the state is reinforced by the giant Nashville-based publishing industry of several church denominations and occasional news items of snake-handlers among the more zealous fundamentalists. Both the figures and the folklore suggest that Tennesseans probably remain closer to the old frontier in their religion than in any other aspect of their lives.

The pulpit has remained a major claim to professional superiority—at least in numbers. By mid-twentieth century, clergymen were the only professional group in which Tennessee was proportionally better supplied than the nation. With proportionally only 75 percent as many doctors, 55 percent as many social workers, and 48 percent as many artists, authors, and ac-

20. John B. Knox, *The People of Tennessee* (Knoxville: University of Tennessee Press, 1949), p. 177.

21. Douglas W. Johnson, Paul R. Picard, and Bernard Quinn, *Churches and Church Membership in the United States* (Washington, D.C.: Glenmary Research Center, National Council of Churches of Christ in the U.S.A., 1974), p. 10.

tors, as the rest of the nation, Tennessee rated 102 percent on clergymen.[22]

It has been said that in the state there was an early, unspoken agreement among the three leading Protestant denominations: the Presbyterians would stay in the cities and towns; the Methodists would take the crossroads and countryside; and the Baptists would go up the dirt roads and hollows. If the divisions have not always worked out quite so precisely as that, the folklore still provides an insight into some of the class distinctions that crept into church affiliations.

Francis Asbury's devotion and Frances Wright's dream, each pursued at incalculable personal sacrifice through physical pain and hardship, remain as twin poles, symbolizing part of Tennessee's and America's commitment. Not all the revivalists shared the attitude of an old man who, when asked, "What did you think of the sermon?"—replied, "Think? I didn't come here to think. I come here to holler."

And not often did Frances Wright succumb to the tart humor and pessimism of her message to a friend: "Co-operation has well nigh killed us all."

Perhaps both more thought and more co-operation were necessary—then and now—to achieve an effective, enduring balance between faith and works, the ideal and the practical, between a paradise in eternity and a heaven here on earth.

22. Knox, *People of Tennessee*, p. 132.

8

Old Lonesome Songs and Jolly Times

*F*ROM the hymns of John Wesley to the protest songs of the 1960s, music has played a vital role in shaping and deepening our national character. Music is as significant to America as gold is to the meaning of wealth, for cities and regions across the country stake their own particular claims to this rich harmonic mine. New Orleans has its jazz and ragtime, Chicago its blues, the midwestern prairie its romantic tradition of cowboy tunes and lonesome wails. And as in so many other fields, New York City attracts and encourages musicians from throughout the United States.

But there is one area which, above all others, has nurtured the fundamental strains of American music. Because of Tennessee's peculiar geographic position, it has known dulcimer makers, bluegrass banjoists, country fiddlers, singers of the blues, guitarists by the thousands, and the very molders of rock and roll.

The story of Tennessee music is a story of people building on the past. In a sequence to be repeated many times over, Tennesseans enjoyed and learned from their sturdy musical heritage, then added to the mainstream their own special contributions and strengths. The ballad makers of East Tennessee drew heavily on Scotch-Irish and English folk songs, yet they "Americanized" these songs and wrote others that reflected the immediate

135

conditions of the New World. The blues singers of West Tennessee grasped hold of Delta chants and southern spirituals and cast a new form to grip the heartland of the Mississippi. Musicians from across the state grew up on the ballads and the blues, gravitated toward Nashville, and discovered their own kind of sound.

The fact that "country" constitutes only a part of this state's vast musical history helps explain why, without much doubt, Tennessee is Eden for the music of the American people. From "The Knoxville Girl," "The Memphis Blues," and "Chattanooga Choo-Choo" to "The Tennessee Waltz," "Jailhouse Rock," and "Nashville Skyline Rag," talented performers and willing audiences have conspired to make that music a growing bond for men and women in the United States and around the world.

The rugged eighteenth-century pioneers of Scotch-Irish and English descent who penetrated through northeastern Tennessee and settled the Unakas, and later the Cumberlands, did so with music at their side. As struggling settlers put down roots in Jonesboro or French Lick or dozens of other stations, they held various community "workings" and celebrated their accomplishments with song and dance. If a log-rolling or a house-raising cleared new land or started a homestead, it also fulfilled other less tangible needs. A man with his guitar might join a fiddler or a neighbor with a banjo and strike up such sociable tunes as "Billy in the Wild Woods" or "Jenny, Put the Kettle On." One favorite with boys and girls was "Buffalo":

Come to me, my dear, and give to me your hand
And let us take a social ramble to some far and distant land
Where the hawk shot the buzzard and the buzzard shot the crow
And we all ride around the canebrake and shoot the buffalo.

As historian Harriette Simpson Arnow suggests, this chant allowed young people to "join hands and go stepping around the circle, happy in the knowing they were committing no sin." [1]

1. Harriette Simpson Arnow, *Flowering of the Cumberland* (New York: Macmillan, 1963), p. 400.

Other songs mirrored the forthright frontier way of life, as well as the adaptability of certain tunes. For instance, one dance number which might say, "Polly, put the kettle on and we'll all have tea," in one area, could change, in another locale, to "Molly, blow the bellows strong, we'll all take tea." Harmonizing fashion and economy was the admonition: "The linsey gown, if you want to keep your credit up, pay the money down." A French harp or jew's-harp might join in on these frolics, but a string instrument called the dulcimer, fashioned from the deep-grained wood of cherry or walnut or sugar maple, was less a joiner than a kind of formal accompanist for the human voice. That voice was soon to be put to heavy use by the singing mountaineers.

Even as the Appalachian pioneers pushed westward on a new continent, they carried with them a bountiful legacy from the islands of old. By memory and word of mouth, East Tennesseans inherited and acted out the racial heritage of Scotland and the British Isles. Ballads sung on cabin porches and before stone hearths brought families and clans together by recreating in song the stirring and sometimes gruesome stories of the past. "Mary Hamilton," for example, tells a tale of intrigue and death in the Scottish court of Mary Stuart. Its power unfolds in the lament of a mother, awaiting execution for the murder of her unwanted child.

The ballads spread throughout the southern Appalachians as quickly as the ridges and valleys were settled. Recent scholars have written of the traditional ballad as impressive and affecting, possessing the germ of poetic life, but it takes no genius to realize that this deep-rooted music strikes basic emotional chords:

> Oh, Lady Sarah she was fair
> But she had lived with sorrow,
> For they have slain her sweetest swain
> In the lonely glens of Yarrow,
> The lonely glens of Yarrow.[2]

2. "In the Lonely Glens of Yarrow," from Sarah Jane Hadley, collected by John Jacob Niles, in *The Ballad Book of John Jacob Niles* (New York: Dover Publications, Inc., 1961), p. 295.

"Mary Hamilton" is a historical ballad; "In the Lonely Glens of Yarrow" tells of a young man killed by his sweetheart's family, yet the event takes second place to the sadness it creates. Other love ballads, such as "Silver Dagger" and "The Jealous Lover," also involve treachery and murder. The supernatural, in the form of ghosts, appears in "Fair Margaret and Sweet William" and "The Wife of Usher's Well," while humorous ballads like "Four Nights Drunk" contain their own ribald brand of attraction. In the latter, the husband stumbles home, to find a strange head on the pillow beside his "pretty little wife," who explains that it is merely a cabbage head given to her by her mother. The befuddled husband muses, plaintively, that he has never before seen a moustache on a cabbage head.

Through the 1800s, the people of the Tennessee hills took the old world songs and adapted them, recreated them with a more American flavor. Or they simply wrote their own, such as "Davy Crockett," a state hero who, according to the song, was "born on a mountaintop in Tennessee." Well-known ballads like "The Elfin Knight" became localized into many variants, such as the Tennessee version called "My Father Gave Me an Acre of Ground." These "American" ballads were often shorter, more lyrical, and more universally dramatic, than the old story-ballads. Their appeal spread into the South and West, but one early twentieth-century observer stated for a fact that "in the mountains singing is more common and universal than in any other area of equal geographic size." [3]

The fervor of religion accounted for a good deal of this music-making. As early as the eighteenth century, special singing schools flourished along with the rural churches. Formal instructors taught the hymns of John Wesley and Isaac Watts, along with sacred folk songs such as "We Have Fathers Gone to Heaven" and "That Deep Settled Peace in My Soul." Many teachers insisted on the "shape note" or "fasola" style of musical notation, in which singers adopted an unusual scale and recognized notes by shape rather than by position. In any case,

---

3. Arthur Palmer Hudson, "Folk Songs of the Southern Whites," in *Culture in the South*, edited by W. T. Couch (Chapel Hill: University of North Carolina Press, 1935), p. 520.

the world of the more secular ballads differed greatly from this restrained atmosphere. A typical set of instructions suggested the following:

> All whispering, laughing, talking, or strutting about the floor in time of school is ridiculous and should not be suffered . . .
> Teachers should sing but a few tunes at a time, and continue to sing them until they are well understood. The parts should be exercised separately until each part could perform their own, before they should be permitted to join in concert.[4]

Be that as it may, the strict teachers of religious music extended its deep influence throughout Tennessee and beyond. Rigdon McCoy McIntosh, born in Maury County in 1836, composed and sang until the end of the century. Christopher Bell, who joined the Confederate Army at the age of fifteen and lost the use of an arm at the Battle of Dalton, Georgia, learned shape-note music and taught at conventions up and down northern Georgia and eastern Tennessee. From 1912 to 1923, Benjamin Unseld helped hundreds of shape-note singers and teachers at the famous Vaughan Conservatory in Lawrenceburg. W. H. Swan of Knoxville wrote many a hymn named after Tennessee communities such as Athens, Holston, and Spring Place.

A musical stimulus of crucial importance was the camp meeting, which captivated the mountain frontier during the Great Revival of the early 1800s. In their frenzy to be saved, participants relied strongly on group singing and choruses. "Singing and praying" opened one 1824 "love feast" in Tennessee's Methodist Holston District. The camp meeting spirituals told of the good life after conversion; they differed from regular hymns through their simplicity and heavy use of repetition:

> We'll stem the storm, it won't be long,
> The heav'nly port is nigh;
> We'll stem the storm, it won't be long,
> We'll anchor by and by.[5]

---

4. William Moore, *Columbian Harmony* (Cincinnati: Morgan, Lodge, Fishon, 1925), quoted in George Pullen Jackson, *White Spirituals in the Southern Uplands* (Chapel Hill: University of North Carolina Press, 1933), p. 45.

5. Dickinson Bruce, *And They All Sang Hallelujah* (Knoxville: University of Tennessee Press, 1974), p. 117.

Such effective choruses soon found their way into tune books. A good many of the important "harmony" compilers came from Tennessee. Working in Nashville, Allen Carden put together the *United States Harmony* in 1829. John Jackson's *Knoxville Harmony* and William Cardwell's *Union Harmony* were published in Maryville and Madisonville during the late 1830s. M. L. Swan brought out his *Harp of Columbia* in 1849 and revised it after the Civil War. These works presented and distributed a spectrum from hymns to sacred ballads to shape-note exercises. And they included legacies from the days of the camp meeting:

> I am bound for the promised land,
> I'm bound for the promised land,
> O, who will come and go with me?
> I am bound for the promised land.[6]

The particular rhythm of this lyric points to a significant phenomenon in the history of Tennessee and American music: the similarity between white and black spirituals and folk songs, and the larger borrowing and mutual development of both. The integrated camp meeting had much to do with this overlap. The sight of blacks and whites together in "singing ecstasies" or the "pen" of converted sinners was not unusual. Black preachers even led occasional meetings and exhorted their white brethren to follow Jesus. It was no accident that a shape-note version of "Roll, Jordan" appeared in an 1820 harmony.

In the years following the Civil War, Reconstruction freedmen drew national attention and interest. Black spirituals received wide popularity and helped finance newly founded schools, such as Nashville's Fisk University. In 1871, a group of eight students calling themselves "The Fisk Jubilee Singers" left on their first concert tour, a tour whose success led to many more. By singing such affecting songs as "Steal Away" and "No Auction Block for Me" before Europe's royalty and America's wealthy, the Jubilee Singers earned hundreds of thousands of dollars for their university. "Swing Low, Sweet

6. John B. Jackson, *The Knoxville Harmony of Music Made Easy* (Madisonville, Tenn.: D & M Shields & Jackson, 1838), quoted in Jackson, *White Spirituals,* p. 48.

Chariot,'' a spiritual sung for Queen Victoria, had its origins along the Cumberland River. A slave mother, grieving for her baby because it had been sold, was about to drown her little daughter and herself. An old woman happened by and dissuaded the mother by saying, "Wait, let the chariot of the Lord swing low, and let me take one of the Lord's scrolls and read it to you." [7]

Tradition has it that the baby grew up, entered Fisk, and became one of the original Jubilee Singers. Even if the lines of descent were not quite so direct as that, blacks preserved and enlarged the musical heritage of their ancestors. As with choruses and spirituals, ballads embraced and benefitted from a blending of black and white. Ballads had spread far out of the mountains, crossing racial lines and witnessing the addition of rascally, lonesome songs such as "The Boll Weevil" or "The Coon-Can Game." In April of 1900, when a young crack engineer named "Casey" Jones wrecked on a run out of Memphis, his black friend Wallace Saunders improvised a singing tribute for the man from Cayce, Kentucky. The separate but related "bad man" ballads recorded the adventures of such notorious characters as "Stagolee," the Memphis gambler who murdered Billy Lyons with his forty-five because of a Stetson hat.

Yet the real music of the black man grew out of all these strains and more. The blues—a feeling, a tremendous mixture of sorrow and joy—arose from three main sources. The first was the ballads, a strong white tradition that merged its elements into early "blues" songs such as "Joe Turner" and "Frankie and Johnnie." The second source was the choruses and hymns, which represented another cultural contact between the worlds of black and white. Black spirituals become more direct and plaintive:

> My Lord delivered Daniel,
> My Lord delivered Daniel,
> My Lord delivered Daniel,
> Why can't he deliver me? [8]

7. B. A. Botkin, editor, *A Treasury of Southern Folklore* (New York: Crown Publishers, 1949), p. 470.

8. Bruce Cook, *Listen to the Blues* (New York: Charles Scribner's Sons, 1973), p. 55.

The third and major source of the blues involved no white musical influence whatsoever. The roots of field songs, hollers, and chants were imbedded in another kind of authority: slavery and, later, economic suppression. The grisly system of discrimination which purposely led to black prison farms, chain gangs, levee crews, and the "milder" forms of day-to-day, back-breaking work unknowingly contributed to a unique singing style, a lasting musical power.

But the people of the Mississippi Delta, the Arkansas cotton fields, and the similar counties of West Tennessee directed their songs at other targets, as well. One 1890s observer noted that the black man "sang about everything: trains, steamboats, steam whistles, sledge hammers, fast women, mean bosses, and stubborn mules." [9] The observer was a man by the name of W. C. Handy. Handy's life in and around Memphis helps show why this area was perhaps the foremost among that collection of American lands that nurtured and popularized the blues.

"Where the Tennessee River, like a silver snake, winds her way through the red clay hills of Alabama, sits high on these hills my home town." [10] So begins William Christopher Handy's autobiography, *Father of the Blues*. He was born on November 16, 1873, in the peaceful town of Florence, just south of the Tennessee line. His father and grandfather were Methodist ministers who "stole an education." As a boy, William did some thieving of his own, for at every opportunity he would steal away to hear the laborers sing along the banks of the Tennessee River.

Strongly attracted to the folk music around him, young Handy encountered obstacles at all sides. In church, his mother frowned on so-called "shout" songs and favored more polite spirituals. His father made him return a hard-earned guitar and trade it in for a *Webster's Unabridged*. His teacher for eleven years, Y. A. Wallace, from Fisk University, drilled pupils in the old "singing school" manner and instructed them in

9. Botkin, *Southern Folklore*, p. 699.

10. W. C. Handy, *Father of the Blues: An Autobiography* (New York: Macmillan, 1941), p. 1.

choruses from Wagner, Bizet, and Verdi. Besides ignoring the material of the Fisk Jubilee Singers, Wallace engaged in other eccentricities. He carried his lunch in his pocket, dined alone, and ate the same thing day after day: "a single baked sweet potato, sliced and buttered." [11]

But Y. A. Wallace introduced W. C. Handy to the rudiments and complexities of music. At the age of fifteen, and without his father's knowledge, Handy paid $2.50 for a used cornet and joined a local band. Four years later, when he graduated, he found himself well-grounded and willing to move mountains. After teaching for a time in the vicinity, Handy discovered that he could make more money at the Howard and Harrison Pipe Works in Bessemer. Once there, he organized a singing quartet and struck out for Chicago with a capitalization of exactly twenty cents.

Although Chicago was hardly a success, W. C. Handy fell in love with the traveling life. He compensated for a dreary stopover in East St. Louis by meeting his future wife in Henderson, Kentucky. Then, in August of 1896, a friend invited him to try out for the famous Mahara's Minstrels. Handy landed a job playing trumpet, and his hopes rose, along with his salary. If the comic entertainment of such minstrel shows did little in the way of serious musical innovation, W. A. Mahara's tours "from Cuba to California, from Canada to Mexico" showed W. C. Handy the breadth of America and the moods of its people.

By 1903, Handy was directing the Knights of Pythias band in Clarksdale, Mississippi. He had come home to play "for affairs of every description," and he "came to know by heart every foot of the Delta." His trained ear sought out, remembered, and enlarged upon the rich melodic offerings around him. Singers and players alike were simply singing and playing, and they "didn't care who knew it." At an engagement in Cleveland, Mississippi, a local group put the Knights to shame by strumming "a kind of stuff that has long been associated with cane rows and levee camps." Wrote Handy: "That night a composer

---

11. Handy, *Father of the Blues*, p. 14.

was born, an *American* composer. Those country black boys in Cleveland had taught me something that could not possibly have been gained from books, something that would, however, cause books to be written.'' [12]

At the age of 32, W. C. Handy moved to Memphis and took over a larger band. Handy had known this city since boyhood and felt particularly at home along one special avenue that wound for a commercial mile through the heart of Memphis. For a decade or more, Beale Street had built a reckless reputation as a center for gambling, whiskey, women, music; it presented an *A*-sharp to Main Street's *G*. When Handy arrived in town, Beale Street presented him to the world.

Politics was the catalyst. In 1909, three men were running for the mayoralty of Memphis. When a ward leader hired Handy's band to push for E. H. Crump, W. C. wrote a tune for the candidate and called it ''Mister Crump.'' The song was a blockbuster. It catapulted Crump to victory and caused actual dancing in the streets. Handy later retitled it ''The Memphis Blues'' and sold it to a Denver businessman. Other Handy hits, such as ''Beale Street Blues'' and ''The Hesitating Blues,'' led him to a successful career as a publisher. W. C. Handy, the rover from northern Alabama, gave lectures by the dozens and even anthologized his songs into a book. He never stopped traveling.

Handy, who died in 1958, was a great synthesizer. He merged the music of his region and the experiences of his own life, ending up with works like ''St. Louis Blues'' and ''Joe Turner Blues.'' Joe Turner—actually Turney—was brother to Peter Turney, governor of Tennessee from 1893 to 1897. Joe was a feared sheriff who sometimes rounded up prisoners in Memphis and returned with them to Nashville. Handy took the popular Tennessee folk song ''Joe Turner,'' magnified its themes, and wrote:

> You'll never miss the water till the well runs dry,
> You'll never miss the water till the well runs dry,
> You'll never miss Joe Turner till he says, ''Goodbye.''

---

12. Handy, *Father of the Blues,* p. 81.

Sometimes I feel like somethin' throwed away,
Yes, sometimes I feel like somethin' throwed away,
And then I get my guitar, play the blues all day.[13]

Just as the mountains of East Tennessee had lured Scotch-Irish and English balladeers down from northern ports or across from the Carolina lowlands, so did Memphis draw bluesmen like W. C. Handy up from the Delta and in from the surrounding countryside. Walter ("Furry") Lewis was born in 1893 in Greenwood, Mississippi, and his family moved to Memphis, six years later. Lewis settled in Memphis and played guitar with the Memphis Jug Band and with Handy himself. Born in Louisiana in 1900, "Memphis Minnie" McCoy grew up in northern Mississippi, sang Beale Street from end to end, then took Chicago by storm. Booker T. Washington ("Bukka") White wrote "Parchman Farm Blues" while serving three years on a Mississippi murder charge; in 1930, he came to Memphis "to stay," at the age of 21.

And there was Fred McDowell, born in 1904 in Rossville, Georgia, reared on his uncle's farm there in Fayette County until he went to live with a sister in Mississippi. Before he died in Memphis in 1972, "Mississippi" Fred McDowell delivered the blues with a master's touch. He even played his "Rambling Blues" for Rhode Island's Newport Folk Festival in 1964. Another participant in the same festival was also born in 1904 in Tennessee. "Sleepy John" Estes grew up near Ripley in Lauderdale County and was discovered on a Memphis street corner by a talent scout for RCA.

The list could go on. Like the traditional ballads, the blues of the early twentieth century found their relentless way into heart and home. From sun-scalded fields to Beale Street and the anonymous alleys of town and city, the blues rained down with an undeniable potency. Along with the ballads, the blues became a major influence on all American music. In the coal country of East Tennessee, both these powerful strains combined to mold the beginnings of yet a third musical force.

13. Dorothy Scarborough, *On the Trail of Negro Folk Songs* (Cambridge, Mass.: Harvard University Press, 1925), p. 266.

In the post-Civil War era, Tennessee's Cumberland Mountains became one of the first extensive coal fields in the entire Southeast. Railroads connected Nashville with Knoxville, pushed into nearby towns, and opened up counties to the north. Coal Creek, in Anderson County, developed as a mining center and boomed, as it shipped tons of coal out of the district. Such prosperity attracted black and immigrant miners, as well as native mountain whites.

In the midst of apparent peace, labor troubles erupted. When, in 1876, the Knoxville Iron Company cut its wage from a nickel to two and a half cents per mined bushel of coal, workers called a strike. The company brought in convicts to continue production. Other companies soon employed convicts by persuading prisons to "lease" the labor of their workers, and the regular miners seethed. Tensions grew until July of 1891; on the anniversary of Bastille Day in France, hundreds of Coal Creek miners stormed the Tennessee Coal Mining Company's Briceville stockade. The miners promptly loaded guards and convicts alike on a Knoxville-bound freight train. A week later, the miners fought off a band of state troopers. Faced with legislative anger, that of the miners passed the boiling point. They burned the Briceville stockade and began simply to release convicts.

All-out war resulted. The conflict spread southward to Marion County, where a stockade was dismantled. By mid-1892, five thousand state troops were in the general region. The next spring, a full-fledged battle took place in Grundy County's Tracy City. But the miners could not hold out indefinitely. Although Coal Creek's conflicts were finally ended in 1896, convicts dug Tennessee coal until World War II.

The town of Coal Creek changed its name to Lake City, but the woes of the coal miners lingered on. Violence, despair, and sheer grit combined and gave rise to such gripping ballads as "Coal Creek Troubles" and "Coal Creek March." The particularly hard life of the coal country also made room for the blues. Black convicts in Tracy City were responsible for the dramatic "Lone Rock Song." [14] As folklorist Archie Green has sug-

14. Archie Green, *Only a Miner: Studies in Recorded Coal-Mining Songs* (Urbana: University of Illinois Press, 1972), p. 208.

gested, blacks and whites alike played together "in local entertainments, medicine shows, carnivals, rural taverns, country
stores . . . Here they would gossip and observe, as well as ab-
sorb the sounds of harmonica and guitar, the poetry of the
blues, the story of a ballad." [15] Charles Bowman, born in 1899
near Johnson City, learned "Nine-Pound Hammer" from listening to the chants of black railroad workers. Bowman remembered the song after boyhood days and recorded it in 1927 as
guitarist for a group called "Al Hopkins and His Buckle Busters."

The "Buckle Busters" sometimes went by another name:
"The Hill Billies." As early as 1900, the *New York Journal* had
reported that a hillbilly "lives in the hills, has no means to
speak of, dresses as he can, talks as he pleases, drinks whiskey
when he gets it, and fires off his revolver as the fancy takes
him." [16] Little did the *Journal* know that its newfound caricatures would soon be setting America's musical pace. For certain
things were happening in hills and hollows, mines and taverns,
fields and homes throughout Tennessee and the South. Musicians, born and reared in the crucible of merging traditions,
were themselves coming together to mold what would in time
be known as country music.

They were recording. Radio burst upon the scene in 1920,
records   a   year   later.   These   two   media   revolution-
ized—industrialized—the music world. Tennesseans such as Uncle Dave Macon and Tom Ashley, who had been traveling
with minstrellike medicine shows, turned to recording and
helped to pioneer the new sound. Clarence Ashley, a Mountain
City native born in 1895, picked his banjo through more than
fifty records before he died in 1967. David Harrison Macon,
who grew up near the Cumberland coal fields, teamed with Sam
McGee in the late 1920s and cut a popular version of the "Lone
Rock Song" called "Buddy, Won't You Roll Down the Line."
And in Bristol, during the first week of August 1927, an RCA
scout named Ralph Peer made the first recordings of the two

---

15. Green, *Only a Miner*, p. 388. Material on Coal Creek taken largely from this
book.

16. The *New York Journal*, April 23, 1900, quoted in Robert Shelton and Burt
Goldblatt, *The Country Music Story* (New York: Bobbs, Merrill, 1966), p. 33.

biggest names in early country: Jimmie Rodgers and the Carter Family.

Radio made an even greater impact on the public than did records. Families who could not afford a phonograph did have the money to buy a crystal set, and they certainly had the time and inclination to hear its offerings. "Barn Dances," "Hayrides," and "Jamborees" could be heard on stations from Chicago to Shreveport, Knoxville to Mexico. These programs mixed music with comedy and, in the style of the old minstrel shows, thought nothing of following "Wildwood Flower" or "Mother Was a Lady" with a joke or two about the mother-in-law and the traveling salesman. Although these shows were popular—and some were extremely so—the blockbuster of them all was begun by a Memphis newspaperman in a tiny Nashville studio.

George D. Hay, a reporter for the *Memphis Commercial Appeal,* happened to love country music. During his newspaper travels, he had enjoyed many an old-fashioned "hoe-down," and, by the 1920s, he was announcing for Chicago's Barn Dance. When Nashville opened a radio station five years later, Hay was there. On October 28, 1925, the opening night of the WSM Barn Dance, he featured a fiddler named Uncle Jimmy Thompson. For the next two years, performers on the show found themselves at the heart of a wide listening audience. Then one Saturday night, just after a program of classical music had left the air, Hay responded with an introduction to his own kind of entertainment: "Ladies and gentlemen, for the past hour we have been listening to music taken largely from Grand Opera, but from now on we will present 'The Grand Ole Opry.' " [17] The Grand Ole Opry became the longest-running radio program in American history. As its popularity leaped, it moved from the small studio to a local movie house, then in 1941 to a former church: historic Ryman Auditorium. The Opry was a major— perhaps *the* major—cause of Nashville's ascent as the Mecca of country music.

17. George Hay, "The Story of the Grand Ole Opry," in Shelton and Goldblatt, *The Country Music Story,* p. 108.

Tennesseans bolstered their thriving stage with dozens of first-rate entertainers. Uncle Dave Macon, otherwise known as "the Squire of Readyville" or "the Dixie Dew-Drop," joined the Opry in 1925 at the age of fifty-five. Writer Robert Shelton has called Uncle Dave "the grandfather of country music," and the title fits. Macon combined comedy, banjo, Jack Daniel's, and a mouth full of gold teeth into a showman's mixture that won audiences for the next quarter-century. The successor to Uncle Dave's early years of stardom was a slim fellow born in 1903 near Maynardsville. Roy Acuff—"the King"—captivated the nation during the rigors of World War II. To many a G.I. on some lonely outpost, Roy Acuff singing "The Great Speckled Bird" came as the voice of home. Singing and playing the fiddle to songs both sacred and secular, Acuff was country music's first real idol and helped to draw America's attention southward.

As with Memphis and the blues, Nashville attracted ambitious men and women from counties to the east and west. Accomplished comedians—Minnie Pearl, Archie Campbell, Homer and Jethro—came in from Centerville, Knoxville, and Bulls Gap. Eddy Arnold, born in 1918 in Henderson, began his career as a radio singer in Jackson; his smooth voice soon took him eastward, where at one time he had nine of the year's top ten records. Chet Atkins, a shy but talented boy from the ballad-making country of East Tennessee, drifted to Nashville by way of Knoxville's WNOX and half a dozen other city stations. Born in 1924 on a fifty-acre Union County farm near Luttrell, Atkins overcame asthma and poverty to become one of Nashville's most influential leaders—and one of the world's most proficient guitarists.

Of all the musicians who gravitated toward Nashville, none ever made a greater impact than Hank Williams. A lean and volatile man, Williams was born in 1923 in an Alabama log cabin. The songs that he wrote during his short life were steeped in the traditions of blues, country, and deeply felt emotion, made specific through his invoked cry of the lonesome whippoorwill and whine of midnight train. When he played for the first time in Ryman Auditorium in June of 1949, Hank Williams gave the Grand Ole Opry one of its most memorable moments. He sang "Lovesick Blues" and six encores, and the audience had to be begged to let him leave the stage. At the age of twenty-nine, Hank Williams died while being driven in his Cadillac to an Ohio performance. After it learned the news, a crying audience sang his "I Saw the Light." The legend of this genuine man lives on, and his songs remain.

Farther to the west, a younger man was making his first record in downtown Memphis. His name was Elvis. Though born in northern Mississippi's East Tupelo, Elvis Presley grew up on both sides of the state line, singing old camp meeting songs and listening to the blues around him. In 1953, when he was eighteen, Elvis left a five-dollar-a-day truck-driving job and made his way to the Sun Records offices in Memphis. At Sun, things went slowly until Sam Phillips heard Elvis really respond during a coffee break to some off-the-cuff homegrown tunes. Phillips recorded such early Elvis hits as "That's All Right" and "Mystery Train," then had them distributed through a new grass-roots technology: the forty-five-rpm juke box.

Elvis's unique style blended rhythm with blues, country with a beat, and singing itself with a striking personality. "Heartbreak Hotel," "Hound Dog," and "Don't Be Cruel" led to dozens of gold records and America's golden age of rock-and-roll. The influence of Elvis on this nation's modern music spread wide and deep, and Tennessee was no exception. Johnny Cash, Jerry Lee Lewis, Charlie Rich, and West Tennessee's Carl Perkins worked in Memphis and helped to merge Elvis's sound with the continuing strains of country and western. Bristol-born Tennessee Ernie Ford even added a rock background to a rather traditional Merle Travis coal song. The "pea-pickin' Plato" recorded "Sixteen Tons" in September of 1955 and saw it sell over four million copies in less than a year.

A new era had arrived, one whose mix of statewide sounds pushed in turn down a variety of avenues. Overton County's Lester Flatt joined the Grand Ole Opry during World War II, then left Bill Monroe's Bluegrass Boys when he met a banjoist named Earl Scruggs. Flatt and Scruggs and their Foggy Mountain Boys played an important part in the development of the bluegrass style. Their music ranged from singing the praises of Martha White flour to telling the Clampetts' televised adventures as "The Beverly Hillbillies." Young musicians in Tennessee and across the country have adopted bluegrass and play it with gusto.

Today, Tennessee music is preserving and building upon its folk traditions. In Memphis, Stax Records carries the banner of soul and features such rhythm-and blues artists as Isaac Hayes and David Porter. Shape-note singing conventions are perennially revived in East Tennessee. And Nashville, with its "sound" that stirs a response across the U.S.A. and around the world, flourishes as the capital of country music. Its recording studios are among the most sophisticated in the entertainment world; its Opryland Museum-playground is a major regional attraction, drawing visitors from far beyond Tennessee.

While Tennessee has produced queens of country music, such as Sevier County's Dolly Parton, and presented dozens of others, such as Loretta Lynn, from neighboring states, it has also sustained symphony orchestras in its four major cities and sent stars to the nation's Metropolitan Opera. There was Grace Moore, born in 1901 in the mountains of Cocke County beside the clear, rushing waters of Big Creek out of the Great Smokies. After a legendary progression from church choir to night club to study abroad to the opera houses of the world, Grace Moore also introduced glamour to grand opera and widened its appeal. Her Mimi and Louise and Tosca were believable heroines, physically as well as vocally. In a movie, *One Night of Love,* she popularized opera and opened at least part of the way for the world's great music to find a larger American audience. An airplane crash as she was returning home from a royal command performance in Scandinavia cut short her life and career at its zenith. There have been others, more recent—such as blonde, warmly personable Mary Costa, from Knoxville, and brunette, highly acclaimed Mignon Dunn, of Memphis—who spanned the distance from Tennessee to the Metropolitan to Covent Garden to La Scala.

When the English folksong collector Cecil Sharp came to Southern Appalachia and East Tennessee, he wrote: "I found myself for the first time in my life in a community in which singing was as common and almost as universal a practice as speaking." [18]

Whether those songs were the plaintive ballads, the troubled spirituals, the militant work songs, the "sinful" blues of yesterday, or the "soulful" rhythms of today, or the classic arias of all time, Tennessee has helped to create and interpret them. There is neither color nor sex, neither age nor class, in the plucked tunes of the dulcimer, the soaring strains of Charpentier. There is the lonely, haunting spirit of humanity here—and everywhere.

18. Couch, editor, *Culture in the South,* p. 519.

9

All Manner of Classrooms

$\mathcal{D}$ID "O.K." originate with Andrew Jackson, who made the notation on a document he wished to approve as "All Correct?"

If not, it could have been so. According to Jackson's biographer, Parton, "Jackson lived at a time when few men and no women could spell." [1]

If not, it should have been so. According to the linguist Bergen Evans, "*O.K.* is probably today the most widely used single term in human speech." [2]

Both the error and its subsequent worldwide popularity are suited to the Jackson legend and the Tennessee image. Certainly the president knew how to spell *all;* one version of the beginning of *O.K.* says it appeared on a bill of sale presented by Jackson and marked "O.R.," for "Order Recorded," with *K* later misread for *R*. Whatever the origin, the story fulfilled the general public's attunement to Jackson popularity and to its suspicions of Tennessee culture. [3]

Classroom and laboratory have provided only part of the means and manners by which Tennesseans educated minds and

1. Goodspeed, *History of Tennessee,* p. 724.

2. Bergen Evans and Cornelia Evans, *A Dictionary of Contemporary American Usage* (New York: Random House, 1967), p. 335.

3. Goodspeed, *History of Tennessee,* p. 724; Evans and Evans, *Contemporary American Usage,* p. 335.

hands, communicated, created and recorded their history, expressed their memories and aspirations. Huddled beside their hearths during long, lonely winter evenings, gathered around the Liar's Bench at crossroads store or county courthouse during hot, lazy summer afternoons, waiting at blacksmith shop or grist mill for horse and mule to be shod or corn to be ground, people perfected an oral tradition of legend and witch-tale, family anecdote and community history. From these roots came much of the vitality and originality of the literature and music of the state.

Hunger for beauty as well as utility turned common folk into artisans who created simple, sturdy furniture of walnut, cherry, pine; wove woolen coverlets of intricate design; pieced colorful quilts with names such as Bonaparte's March, Goose Track, Double Wedding Ring; fashioned baskets of white oak and cane and dyes extracted from roots and barks, in ways learned from Indian neighbors; wrought iron into elegant, useful designs and objects; whittled out whimmydiddles and thingamabobs in whimsical playfulness.

In "mansions" scattered across the state, usually surrounded by fertile acres that could support architects, decorations, and objects of art imported from Philadelphia, New York, and Europe, there was evidence of the cultural ties with countries and traditions from which these people had descended.

There was also the contribution of the black imagination and labor. Slavery had cut a whole people away from their racial heritage, but in language, songs, and certain customs, part of that memory was kept alive, became an integral enrichment of the cultural whole. It was black artisans who created much of the complex and enduring masonry in stone and brick. In woodworking, building, and decorating what was required, what was requested, they constructed everything from rude, useful smokehouses to carved bannisters gracing a sweep of stairway.

With this deep current of creativity running through the life of the people, there was also a strong undertow of destructiveness. It was a tug-of-opposites, an ambivalence as old as America, as ancient as the human race, but it seemed to find heightened expression in many phases of Tennessee life.

Perhaps it is necessary to look at the beginning. In Tennessee, as in an earlier garden place, there was the Cain and the Abel: violence and husbandry attending the earth together. There was the brawler impeding the builder, the destroyer vying with the healer, the greedy atavist struggling against the creator searching for bounty of body, mind, and spirit. In its culture as in so much else, Tennessee was again a border state, part of east and west, bearing both the hazards and the tolls of westering.

The pioneers and the drifters came together to Tennessee, as they did to the rest of the Western frontier: one energetically seeking permanence, property, establishment of law; the other shiftlessly scavenging on red and white neighbors, on the earth's plenty, avoiding effort, often evading the law.

One viewpoint reached for civilization, the stability of schools, churches, literature, arts of the mind and crafts of the hand. The other settled for satisfaction, responding to needs by random impulse, foraging for each new gratification. In this casual and often wasteful solution, violence was commonplace: violence of gun and torch, of axe and saw, eventually of bulldozer and pollutant, destroying riches of human and natural resources. The continuing tension was between those who held some sense of what is called "beloved community" and those who lack such awareness; between responsibility and irresponsibility, cooperation and anarchy.

Romantic interpreters on the one hand and revisionist historians on the other have sometimes failed to recognize both of these attitudes, these dual characters which, from the first, were, each, part of the state's development and destiny. Yet only by acknowledging these twin poles that made the frontier destructive as well as constructive, cherishing mediocrity as well as excellence, can we understand some of the surface contradictions and deep paradoxes characteristic of both the past and present.

Early recreation and justice reflected the harshness, often the brutality, of the frontier. Wrestling matches and boxing bouts might involve eye-gouging and biting off pieces of ear or nose. Practical jokes could leave their subject injured or crippled. Hunting was both necessity and pleasure, while cock-fighting, horse-racing, and contests of physical strength were popular pastimes. Duelling was for keeps, as Andrew Jackson proved.

A man who took another man's life—or horse—was usually hanged, especially in the latter case. Occasionally, a horse thief would merely be punished, but the punishment might make him wish he had been dispatched quickly: confinement with both ears nailed to the pillory for an hour, after which the ears were severed; thirty-nine lashes "well laid on," and branding with an *H* on one cheek and *T* on the other. Theft of a horse on the frontier equalled loss of automobile and tractor and boon companion, all in one package.

Public whippings, brandings, and hangings attracted throngs of viewers. Stern moralists often considered it therapeutic for children as well as adults to witness such punishments. The attitude and demeanor of the victim, especially one on the scaffold, was carefully noted by the audience and discussed later as an example of one "hardened" against all redemption or "repentant" in the face of eternity.

Severity of punishment for certain crimes sometimes led juries to avoid returning verdicts of guilty, leaving justice thwarted by the very means meant to promote it. But no improvement in the state's penal code was introduced until the 1820s, when Governor William Carroll, an especially enlightened leader of the state, suggested revision, and the construction of a penitentiary. In 1829, the penitentiary was built, and the public whipping-post and pillory were abolished.

But violence remained part of the fabric of Tennessee life. It was even reflected in correspondence, especially where political campaigns were concerned. One Alfred Balch, writing from Nashville to James K. Polk in 1834, concerning a political opponent, said: "But if his friends will have war we shall return it with the knife and the knife to the hilt." [4]

Literary exaggeration paled beside the bloody statistics of some of the flamboyant cities. Nature's wildness in woods and fields no longer held the mortal danger of man's wilderness ex-

---

4. James K. Polk, *Correspondence of James K. Polk,* edited by Herbert Weaver and Paul H. Bergeron (Nashville: Vanderbilt University Press, 1972), 2:294.

panding in his cities. In 1909, the *Memphis Commercial Appeal* informed its readers: "Killing is now the most thriving industry in this part of the country." [5] During the decade 1900 to 1910, the national homicide rate of cities was 7.2 percent per 100,000 population. For Memphis, the rate was 47.1 percent. By 1918, an insurance company official had labeled Memphis the nation's "murder capital."

Although the statistics had improved by mid-century, the old image was revived by the assassination of Dr. Martin Luther King, Jr., in 1968. The minister and civil rights leader and Nobel Prize winner had come to Memphis to help settle a strike of the city's garbage workers. Standing on the balcony outside his motel room, he was shot and killed. News of his death shocked the world, prompted some to riot, and brought many to mourn. While neither the victim nor his convicted assassin was a Memphian, the event turned world attention to the city and led one Southern reporter to write: "Memphis is America in microcosm. The sickness which led to the death of Dr. King can lead to the death of the United States. The only atonement for this murder, the only hope of national survival, is fast, full action to remedy the wrongs of racism." [6]

Guns have been part of Tennessee life—and death—from the days of the long rifle to the Saturday-night special. They have been symbols of freedom and weapons of fear. They have destroyed wantonly and been brought to their nation's service. During World War I, a farm boy named Alvin York, from Fentress County in Tennessee, became America's hero, the epitome of the civilian-soldier. Separated from his detachment during the Battle of Argonne Forest, York staged a one-man offensive against the German army: he killed twenty enemy soldiers and captured 132 others and marched them back to the American lines. His reappearance there—a lone corporal herding a long line of prisoners—caused something of a sensation. Later, he explained that he had always been a good squirrel-hunter back

5. Miller, *Mister Crump,* p. 30.

6. Wilma Dykeman and James R. Stokely, *The Border States,* Library of America Series (New York: Time-Life Books, 1968), p. 80.

in his Cumberland Mountains. He was promoted to sergeant and received the country's highest awards.

Tennesseans have fought over politics. One editor, Edward Ward Carmack, who had served as U.S. Congressman and Senator, ran for governor in 1908 against incumbent Malcolm Patterson. The race was inflamed by the whiskey issue.

Before the outcome could be determined at the polls, prohibitionist Carmack was killed in a shoot-out on a Nashville street. Duncan Cooper was found guilty, but because of the inflamed atmosphere surrounding the trial, he was pardoned. Governor Patterson was re-elected; his pardon of Carmack's killer remained a subject of heated debate.

Tennesseans have fought over the land and its resources, too; over coal and a decent wage to gouge it out of the black depths of the earth, as seen in the Coal Creek wars; over tobacco and a decent price for its back-breaking, sweat-drenched cultivation and harvest. During a brief, bitter period between 1906 and 1908, the so-called Black Patch Wars spilled over from Kentucky into the north-central Tennessee counties, where prices on dark-leaf tobacco had been forced to rock-bottom by the powerful and unchallenged Tobacco Trust dominated by North Carolinian Buck Duke's huge American Tobacco Company. Desperate farmers joined a Protective Association and then small vigilante groups to boycott the trust, destroy its warehouses and factories, and loosen its stranglehold on the economy of the area's farms. In the end, the Night Riders were overcome by military force, but tobacco prices were improved.

So, too, with the rights to Reelfoot Lake, a contest between a private land company and public ownership, which culminated in the desperate violence of Night Riders seeking remedies outside the law for their accumulated grievances.

On the night of October 21, 1908, the vigilantes—small farmers, fishermen, and hunters in the area—kidnapped two prominent attorneys and shareholders in a land company that controlled Reelfoot Lake and planned to develop it for profit, "to the exclusion of all others." When one of the lawyers would not promise to return former fishing rights to local residents, he was shot. His companion plunged into a nearby bayou, where he narrowly escaped death beneath a rain of shotgun and rifle fire. Five years and many courtrooms later, Reelfoot came under full and legal control of the state.

Paul J. Vanderwood, writing in 1969 of the human and legal upheaval surrounding the final disposition of this lake created by a strange and gigantic upheaval of nature, pointed out: "The animosity spawned between Lake and Obion Counties during the night-riding era left a residue which is evident today. The Obion side of the lake is often referred to as 'Night Rider country,' and visitors are warned not to cross the natives." Change and the calender nullify even murder, however. Mr. Vanderwood notes that "time, motels, communications, and profits are eroding the attitudes that for so long shielded the district from modernization." He concludes that "The trend toward updated living is irreversible" as "younger entrepreneurs welcome both visitors and business." [7]

The coexistence of hospitality and hostility has been part of Tennessee's ambivalence. A wit could refer to the state as observing "the pure feud law," while a Supreme Court Justice could say, following a visit in 1962, that he remembered Tennessee families he met as "the kindest, most thoughtful, most generous people I have known. At the same time they were the proudest and most independent." [8] Strangers might try to "solve" the apparent contradiction of these descriptions, while Tennesseans simply acknowledge each as part of the human condition.

The conflict that has been most costly—and sometimes violent—in the most ways, has involved the profound difference between those pioneers and drifters, those builders and scavengers, those responsible and irresponsible, in their relation to Tennessee education. Schools. Their presence or absence. Learning. Its nourishment or starvation. Perhaps this is one of the most continuous, most neglected, and most gripping dramas

---

7. Paul J. Vanderwood, *Night Riders of Reelfoot Lake* (Knoxville: University of Tennessee Press, 1969).

8. William O. Douglas, "The People of Cades Cove, Tennessee," *National Geographic*, 122, no. 1 (July 1962).

of Tennessee history, joined in more recent conflict than most citizens realize. It engages attitudes carried over from a chaotic past into a complex present.

Although Tennessee's first settlers apparently enjoyed a high rate of literacy (more than 95 percent in some communities), immediate demands of the wilderness and arrival of more abject, wretched contingents along the frontier valued physical prowess above intellectual achievement. Surrounded by forests to be cleared, red tribes to be ameliorated or exterminated, wild animals to be destroyed, and everything for human survival, contentment, and enlightenment yet to be built, muscle ruled over mind. Even the educated and their descendants often acquiesced to the view that education was not only unnecessary but "something effete, not quite becoming to men of virility." Tennessee historian T. P. Abernethy has judged: "One of the most lasting and pernicious byproducts of the frontier is this underrating of education and culture in American life." [9]

Necessity dictated that early pioneers should work for the present and provide for the future. Finally, preoccupation with the here and now, and anticipation of tomorrow, became a habit. Uses of the past, the intellectual heritage of other times and cultures, came to seem a demanding bore or a tedious luxury. Wealthy Tennesseans might send their sons to one of the great universities in the northeast, after they had been tutored at home or in one of the small private academies, but their numbers were limited. Schools were hard-won. Support for the mind's discipline never aroused the enthusiasm surrounding those camp meetings for the soul's salvation. Even today, Tennessee ranks forty-sixth in the nation in its total public school expenditure per pupil.[10] It is well to note, however, that it ranks twenty-fourth in the nation in state funds spent for education.

Yet no single pattern applied to all those who helped open and build Tennessee. There were degrees of difference, and the exceptions stand out with brilliant clarity. Consider, for instance, those two heroic figures, Daniel Boone and Sam Houston.

9. Abernethy, *Frontier to Plantation,* p. 161.
10. *National Education Association Report,* January 1975.

Boone had knowledge of a very real and practical kind, but he would probably have frowned upon the romantic description of one of his biographers: "Though unacquainted with books, Boone had perused certain parts of the great volume of nature with diligent attention." [11]

This was one sort of learning, certainly, but Sam Houston apparently understood the necessity for acquaintance with more formal volumes. While attending school, Houston memorized Pope's translation of Homer's *Iliad* almost in its entirety. Then he asked to be taught Greek and Latin. When his teacher refused, Houston left school and soon disappeared to live among the Cherokees, where he grew to manhood. In 1811, at the age of eighteen, he returned and opened a school in the present Blount County. His tuition charge was eight dollars a year, payable one third in cash, one third in corn, and one third in cotton cloth. The school disbanded when he went to fight at Horseshoe Bend with Andrew Jackson, in the War of 1812. While still a Tennessean, before departing for Texas, Houston led a delegation of Cherokees to Washington, D. C. In the capital city, he was accused and tried on charges of too much zeal in seeking abolition of the African slave trade through Florida. Later, he returned to study (of law), to the Cherokees (among whom he was known as "The Raven"), and to antislavery (refusing, as governor of Texas, to join the Confederacy). A strange, interesting combination of scout and scholar, woodsman and humanitarian, Sam Houston balanced Homer with humor and represented a sense of the total community of man, even in the rough-hewn little schoolhouse where he taught.

Such log schoolhouses were not plentiful. Public education did not come early or easy to Tennessee. Its appeal was limited—less emotional than religion, less exciting than politics. Its necessity was not immediately apparent. But there were those who sought to fill the need by establishing private academies.

It was the College of New Jersey at Princeton, later Princeton University, that provided the strongest influence on Tennessee's early educational institutions. Three of its graduates came into

11. A. K. Moore, *The Frontier Mind*, p. 195.

the country of the Western Waters with books instead of guns, promoting speculation in ideas rather than land.

Samuel Doak, who sent the over-mountain men to Kings Mountain with a thundering invocation for victory, founded Martin Academy, the first regular school west of the Allegheny Mountains, in 1785. Ten years later, the Academy was chartered as Washington College.

Also in 1785–1786, Thomas Craighead became the head of Davidson Academy, a forerunner of the University of Nashville and George Peabody College for Teachers. Hezekiah Balch's school, known as Greeneville College, was chartered in 1794; later it would become part of the present Tusculum College. The Reverend Messrs. Doak, Craighead, and Balch were all alumni of Nassau Hall, and brought to their raw little institutions on the frontier a dedication to Latin and Greek, public oratory, and private morality.

At their Constitutional Convention in 1796, Tennesseans made no provision for public education. The system of private academies was encouraged and became so entrenched that, by 1889, more than 500 had been chartered for the state. Many of these perished after a few years. Others grew and expanded their role. Chief among the latter was Blount College, established in Knoxville in 1794, one of the first nonsectarian and coeducational schools chartered in the United States. Its name honored territorial governor William Blount, whose daughter Barbara was a student. After undergoing a series of changes, Blount College eventually became the University of Tennessee, with campuses expanding from Knoxville to Memphis.

A forerunner of Maryville College had been established in 1802, as the "log-cabin school" of the Reverend Isaac Anderson. Mr. Anderson, however, was an outspoken Presbyterian minister whose political views were controversial: a seminary was established in 1819, but a charter was not granted until 1842. From its inception, Maryville College excluded no one "by reason of their race or color."

By 1857, the Episcopalians were bringing the English tradition in education to the town of Sewanee with their University of the South, but destruction during the Civil War called for complete reorganization and rebuilding in 1876.

Other institutions of higher education came after the war. There was concern for the Negroes who had had no previous educational establishment. Fisk University was founded by the American Missionary Association of New York and the Western Freedmen's Aid Commission of Cincinnati, and Meharry Medical College was established by the Methodist Episcopal Church. More than 1,200 black students enrolled at Fisk during its first two years.

General O. O. Howard, who remembered that Abraham Lincoln had said he wished to do something for the loyal Unionists of East Tennessee when the Civil War was over, helped establish a college at Harrogate, on the state's northeastern border. It was named Lincoln Memorial University.

Cornelius Vanderbilt, with his millions, was induced to look south. The wife of energetic Methodist Bishop Holland McTyeire was a cousin of Mrs. Vanderbilt's. The Bishop was engaged in a Herculean effort to build up a first-rate university in his city and state, and during a visit to the New York tycoon in 1873 McTyeire presented his plans and a plea for support. He returned home with the pledge of Vanderbilt money—and a new name for the university.

In the struggle for survival during Reconstruction and the long lean years that followed, black colleges were separate and usually starved for funds. Women's schools were also separate (despite Barbara Blount's early example) and anemic in content. A director of one Female Academy summed up his approach: "We educate the girl according to God's word and the demand of every fiber of her mind to be a wife, to be a mother. Then in after life, circumstances determining, she may do anything a female body, mind, and soul may do." [12]

One thing many female bodies, minds, and souls could do was teach—often for low pay, little respect, and grievous hardship. But even that was not possible until the state began to achieve some semblance of public education. Here the quiet subversion wrought by apathy and indifference was difficult to overcome.

Goodspeed's early *General History of Tennessee* considers

12. Federal Writers' Project, *Tennessee: A Guide to the State*, p. 122.

some important contrasts in the educational heritage of early Virginia and North Carolina—of which Tennessee was then part—and the New England colonies. As early as 1637, "the Puritan colonies" were ordering any township that had as many as 100 households to set up a grammar school to fit youth for the university. "In these colonies the fundamental idea was universal education, beginning with the common school and ending with the university. In North Carolina, Tennessee, and other Southern States, the system was reversed. The college was first provided for, leaving the individual to prepare himself for receiving its benefits." Goodspeed then asserts that "the common school, the great preserver of democracy," did not flourish where there was slavery, because there was the feeling that labor needed no intelligence and culture belonged only to the master. "The intermediate class of persons—those who did not own slaves and who were not owned as slaves—occupied a most unfortunate position." Where common schools were established, they did not flourish "in company with the institution of slavery." Public schools were looked upon as "pauper schools." [13]

Thus, there were some extraordinarily well-educated Tennesseans—and many who were illiterate. Acts passed by the U.S. Congress and by the state legislature from 1806 until 1850 set aside lands or funds that were intended for the support of public education. But there was neither the will nor the way to translate such acts into action. When a state-financed system of common schools finally went into effect in 1839, apportioning 62½ cents to each child of school age, the result was not auspicious: the first Superintendent of Public Instruction—engaged in two or three different businesses, as well as education—speculated with the school funds and lost more than $120,000, at that time an impressive sum.

When the census of 1840 was taken, Tennessee discovered that almost one fourth of its adult white population could neither read nor write. It was stung at being "made the subject of sneering remark in almost every newspaper in the country."

13. Goodspeed, *History of Tennessee*, p. 421.

It was Andrew Johnson, illiterate himself until he was a grown man, married, and a tailor in Greeneville, who finally made public education work in Tennessee. In his governor's message to the legislature in 1853, he admitted the inadequacy of common schools and asserted that the only way to educate the children of the state was to ''levy and collect a tax from the people of the whole State.'' There were powerful opponents. But the following year a bill for direct taxation was passed. The first levy of its kind in Tennessee, it has been called ''one of the most constructive contributions to the growth of democracy.'' [14]

Johnson's lifelong consciousness of class probably inspired much of his concern for public schools. Education, or its lack, was the source of hostility, suspicion, and conflict among people who had every other reason to be united rather than divided. In the face of those who sought excuses rather than a remedy for illiteracy, Andrew Johnson's practical, persistent efforts were especially remarkable. As one historian has written, ''The antebellum South produced no other man who could rank with Johnson as a spokesman of the people; one who had their point of view and worked unceasingly and genuinely in behalf of their interests. It is curious that he stands so alone in this role and that his reputation has profited so little from the real work of his life.'' [15]

Shortly after the direct taxation bill was passed, provisions were made for women to be employed on an equal footing with men teachers. Teachers' examinations were also standardized. And it is interesting to note that it was under Governor Andrew Johnson's leadership that a state library was established.

Johnson County (not named for Andrew, but for a Postmaster General under President Polk) became the first county to establish a public school under this taxation law. In 1855, Nashville opened the first public graded school. Three years later, Memphis incorporated its city schools. Public education was just beginning to take root—and then the Civil War came.

14. Abernethy, *Frontier to Plantation,* p. 318.
15. Abernethy, *Frontier to Plantation,* p. 316.

Teachers and students left books for battlefields. Buildings of many private institutions were destroyed or made into hospitals and camps.

When shooting ceased, the uphill struggle for public education began all over again. In addition to the numbers of whites who could neither read nor write, there were now nearly 300,000 newly freed blacks who were in bondage to illiteracy and a segregation that would soon begin to take shape. A weary, burdened public was in no mood—and had scant means—to burden itself with taxes for common schools. Suggestion that some of those schools might be for Negroes was violently opposed. A later journalist, commenting on the fact that carpetbaggers seemed more popular than schoolteachers throughout the South, decided, "We would rather be robbed than improved." [16]

The state superintendent reported that threats of personal violence were forcing teachers to resign. "In July, 1869, sixty-three counties reported thirty-seven schoolhouses had been burned. Teachers were mobbed and whipped; ropes were put around their necks, accompanied with threats of hanging; ladies were insulted." [17] Where classes did survive, the buildings, often log, were mere remnants of better days. Many summer classes were held under the shade of trees.

When the legislature passed a law in 1867 attempting a coherent and adequate state system of public instruction, its efforts were nullified by citizens' apathy and opposition. The state superintendent sadly diagnosed the trouble: "An active popular sympathy is essential to the success of any system of public instruction." [18] By 1872, it could be estimated that not one fifth of the school-age population of the state had any means of education, and in some counties there was not a single school, public or private, in operation.

Private philanthropy helped bridge this terrible gap. The Pea-

16. Jonathan Daniels, *A Southerner Discovers the South,* American Scene, Americana Series (1938; reprint ed., New York: Plenum Publishing Corp., 1970).

17. Goodspeed, *History of Tennessee,* p. 432.

18. Goodspeed, *History of Tennessee,* p. 436.

body Fund in particular kept many schools alive. The Freedmens Bureau provided funds that built most of the early schools for black children. Eventually a group of "friends of popular education" from every part of Tennessee united under the name of the Tennessee State Teachers' Association, and proposed a system based on some standards of equality and excellence, combining features of old state, county, and district systems. The proposal was enacted into law in March 1873, and the public schools were once more on the steep climb out of oblivion.

It would be twenty years before the legislature provided for tax-supported secondary schools, and six years after that before county courts could set up county high schools. By 1909, however, one fourth of Tennessee's revenue was allotted to education. For the next half-century, Tennessee's low per capita income, compared with that of many states of other regions, meant that Tennessee would continually have to run just to stand still. Segregation of white and black meant a double burden of handicap on the latter, whose receipts never equalled those of their white counterparts.

By 1930, the gap between white and Negro schools reflected the wrenching disparities intensified by the Great Depression. World War II helped solve some of the black employment problems—at least momentarily—but the social challenges remained. In 1945, Tennessee was part of that South that emerged from the war, as one resident said, with more social change and more unfinished business than any other part of the country.

Part of that unfinished business included education. In 1954, voiding the old separate-but-equal doctrine, the U.S. Supreme Court ordered school desegregation "with all deliberate speed." Tennessee again emerged as a border state—and as three states. Reaction ranged from compliant to recalcitrant. At Oak Ridge, the high school was quietly desegregated under federal fiat. Seven miles away, in the town of Clinton, tension mounted in the fall of 1956 until the National Guard was called in by Governor Frank Clement. The climax was reached a while later, when integrated Clinton High School was dynamited and destroyed. Citizens across the United States sent funds to help rebuild the school. The segregation cause at Clinton was finally defeated by its own destructiveness.

In schools, at voting booths, in public accommodations, in businesses, in residential areas—all across the spectrum of daily living—black citizens reached for their rights in the 1960s and '70s. There was response—and delay, setback—and progress. According to the 1970 census, the poverty rate among white Tennesseans was 15.3 percent; among black citizens, 38 percent.[19] As one native wryly observed, "In poverty, the black is a little more equal than others."

On the other hand, in 1964, NAACP lawyer A. W. Willis, Jr., was elected to the legislature, the first black to be sent to the General Assembly in the twentieth century. Two years later, he was joined by six other Negroes. One of these was Dr. Dorothy Brown, the first black woman ever to serve in the Tennessee legislature. And in the 1974 elections, a black Representative, Harold E. Ford, was chosen to go from Memphis to the U.S. Congress. Perhaps he and other black political leaders in the state, supported by a growing black middle class, will help find answers to inequities and problems that afflict blacks most heavily but affect all the state. Thus we come full circle to education, to the implications of that figure cited earlier, placing Tennessee forty-sixth in the nation in its total educational expenditures per pupil.

During the early days of Washington College, public antagonism toward "useless" curricula was voiced by one newspaper correspondent who sent a poem to the *Knoxville Intelligencer:*

> When boys have learn'd that they are made
> To heave the earth with plough and spade;
> And girls, that they must toil for man,
> Make clothes, wash pots, and frying pan;
> They're then prepar'd for learning.[20]

But doughty, dogmatic old Samuel Doak had founded Washington College. He valued learning and the books that were its tools. When he came into the Back Country, he brought with

---

19. Southern Regional Council, *The Other 20 Percent*, p. 11.
20. Federal Writers' Project, *Tennessee: A Guide to the State*, p. 295.

him the first books in the Tennessee wilderness. They rode safely ensconced on his only horse's back—while he walked. He was not about to yield up culture to spades and frying pans.

Tennessee began to produce books of its own. But first, there were newspapers. In 1791, a newspaper was established, the *Knoxville Gazette,* with a New Englander, George Roulstone, as its editor. Published for a short while at Rogersville, it soon moved to the town whose name it bore. This was but the first of many papers which would be at the center of stormy political debate and local controversy. Mark Twain, whose family moved from Jamestown, Tennessee, to Missouri only a short while before he was born, returned to the state after he was grown and wrote an uproarious account of fist fights, duels, and horse-whippings among editors. By the time of the Civil War, Nashville was considered the publishing center of the South, with more publications than any other city of its size.

A number of scholarly local historians were at work. John Haywood, of Nashville, who was also a justice of the State Supreme Court, and J. G. M. Ramsey, of Knoxville, who was also a physician, and A. W. Putnam, of Nashville, who was also a lawyer and businessman, each compiled exhaustive studies of various aspects of Tennessee's early days. During the next century, Judge Samuel Cole Williams, of Johnson City, enlarged the state's historical resources.

The sharp contrast in life experience and literary style was illustrated by the works of two early novelists of Tennessee: George Washington Harris and Charles Egbert Craddock—or Mary Noailles Murfree.

Harris, who lived in Knoxville during the mid-nineteenth century, came out of the tradition of Davy Crockett's exuberant *Autobiography* and the yarns spun by long hunters and woodsmen. In this world of swagger and exaggeration, jokes and lie-swapping, Harris created one of the earliest realistic characters in the state's fiction. *Sut Lovingood Yarns,* published in 1867, presented Sut, a "Nat'ral Born Durn'd Fool," narrating adventures of his assorted friends—hunters, farmers, fiddlers, sheriffs, preachers, politicians, and "willin' widders." These were the common folk of the countryside, the crossroads, the little county seats, as they worked and quarreled, played tricks and pulled rusties, devised amusements that were often impudent, sometimes boorish, occasionally painful. Sut Lovingood reflected the frontier capacity to render hardship endurable by mocking it with humor. He was coarse, shrewd, quick, and tough, engaged in a running warfare with hypocrisy and sentimentality, especially as they were embodied (or embalmed) in law and religion. There was hurt in many of his brutal pranks; there was healing in his belly laughs.

Sut Lovingood was a descendant of the great scamps, the Till Eulenspiegels of world literature, and he was an ancestor of the boisterous Americans created in the fiction of Mark Twain (who reviewed *Sut Lovingood Yarns* for a San Francisco newspaper), Erskine Caldwell, Thomas Wolfe, and William Faulkner (who acknowledged the influence of author George Harris). Harris died two years after his book was published. He fell ill on a train trip between Virginia and Alabama and was taken from the train at Knoxville. Just before he died he whispered one word, "Poisoned." There was no autopsy. Was he the victim or the perpetrator of one last grand joke?

Separated by only a few years in time and the distance between East and Middle Tennessee in miles, the difference in spirit between George Harris and Charles Egbert Craddock suggested a chasm. Craddock was, in reality, Mary Noailles Murfree, the sheltered daughter of a central Tennessee planter, who assumed a man's name when she began to write for the *Atlantic Monthly*. Her stories for that magazine won an early and enormous national popularity. Among the books that followed were *Drifting Down Lost Creek, In The 'Stranger People's' Country,* and *The Prophet Of the Great Smoky Mountains* (1885)—and they, too, found a large audience.

Mary Murfree was no realist in the sense that George Harris was, but neither was she a total sentimentalist, as were many of her contemporaries. She wrote of the mountain people among whom she had spent her summers at Beersheba Springs and Montvale Springs and the surrounding countryside, and they became more than the caricatures that they had been judged to be in most previous publications. If she did not caricature, Mary

Murfree did romanticize. Descriptions of cloud-wreathed mountains, rosy sunsets, and limpid streams, phonetic renditions of a dialect that veered from the droll to the tedious, all place Murfree's books in the local-color tradition. She sought authenticity in her stories of mountain moonshiners and their daughters, hard-pinched farmers and their toiling wives, all the pathos of the lonely, frustrated lives of the mountaineers and the solemn poetic beauty of their surroundings. But she worked in a Victorian literary straitjacket that could not admit the full spectrum of life experience or literary expression.

By the 1920s, other native voices were creating a fiction faithful to a variety of Tennessee experiences. T. S. Stribling, of Clifton, drew on his knowledge of the country bordering on the North Alabama hills to write his first novel, *Birthright,* published in 1922, and *The Store,* which won the Pulitzer Prize in 1932. He wrote a half-dozen books, in between. Evelyn Scott combined deep interest in the interior landscape of emotions with the exterior setting of her native Clarksville and countries abroad in works ranging from *The Wave,* a 1929 novel, to *Background In Tennessee,* an autobiography published in 1937. When Roark Bradford, of Memphis and New Orleans, wrote about Negro life, he captured a rich sense of language and folklore, nowhere more evident than in *Ol Man Adam and His Chillun,* published in 1928, which became the basis for Marc Connelly's immensely popular play, *Green Pastures.*

The most important literary development of this period—the 1920s—in Tennessee, however, was the rise of a group called the Fugitives, and, later, the Agrarians. Actually, they were both: fugitives seeking middle ground between ''a sentimentalized South and a commercialized South,'' hoping to preserve some of the best of an agrarian past in an increasingly technological present.

In 1922, a group of sixteen poets organized at Vanderbilt University and published the first issue of a magazine, *The Fugitive.* Under the leadership of John Crowe Ransom, Donald Davidson, Merrill Moore, Allen Tate, and Robert Penn Warren, the little magazine during its three years of life helped nurture the Southern renascence it represented. Its quality remained consistent and its influence increased throughout the publication of its nineteen issues.

The Fugitives dissolved into the Agrarians, twelve young writers whose base was Vanderbilt University. Their leading figures included the Fugitive nucleus of Ransom, Warren, Davidson, and Tate, along with Andrew Lytle, Stark Young, John Gould Fletcher, Frank L. Owsley, Lyle Lanier, H. C. Nixon, John D. Wade, and Henry B. Kline. They represented some of the most articulate talent of the South, and the manifesto they published in 1930 aroused regional and national debate. *I'll Take My Stand* was a collection of twelve articles, in which each contributor considered some aspect of an "Agrarian versus Industrial" way of life. They viewed the Southern past as an ideal represented by the small farmer, independent, self-sufficient, close to the earth and his own humanity. They looked upon the American present as a wasteland of technological progress laden with threats of increasing centralization in politics and standardization in culture. Their solution was a return to the agrarian tradition.

Reaction to this credo revealed the deeply conflicting forces at work in Tennessee, the South, and indeed the nation, as people sought renewed prosperity while cherishing many of the old values, wished to solve rank social injustices while encouraging cultural vitality. Those who felt that the Agrarians were indulging in fruitless nostalgia labeled them "young Confederates," who were "the champions of a second Lost Cause." Those who advocated more direct confrontation of the region's deep-seated health and educational needs of the early 1930s asked, "Are they unaware of pellagra and hookworm, two flowers of Southern agrarianism?"

The Agrarians launched important and fundamental debate. Many of the issues they raised continue to require attention. Most of the dozen participants went on to achieve individual distinction in their fields, ranging from poetry to political science. For a little while, they made a corner of Tennessee the focal point for a lively and significant examination of some of Tennessee's and America's literary, social, and philosophic alternatives.

Continuing contributions to literature reflected Tennessee's variety. Caroline Gordon, of Clarksville, was a stylist whose subject range included the antebellum South in *Penhally*, early frontier struggles in *Green Centuries*, and the natural outdoors- man and gentleman in *Alex Maury, Sportsman*. In contrast, Mildred Haun, born in East Tennessee but a later resident of Nashville, published only one book, *The Hawk's Done Gone*. A collection of stories gathered into the framework of a novel, this was a unique work, rendering the dark terror—relieved by brief moments of humor and beauty—that suffused life in certain isolated mountain coves. In its rhythms, dialect, and folkways, the book was as original and sturdy as an intricately woven cov- erlet of hand-carded wool.

There was terror of another kind in George W. Lee's novel, *River George*. The tension and tragedy in this story, set in Memphis and the surrounding plantation country, grew from the racial pressures welling up beneath an old and accepted suppres- sion. Its author was as interesting as any of his characters. A lieutenant in World War I, he was known along his Beale Street, about which he had written a book, as Lieutenant Lee. For decades, he was a political leader among the minority of blacks in his area who were Republican. To many, he repre- sented a shrewd kind of wisdom or cynicism, depending on the viewpoint, personally accommodating to a world he sought to change.

Between hill-bound upland and river-washed lowland, Middle Tennessee found one voice in novelist Madison Jones, and an- other in Randall Jarrell, an influential teacher, poet, and critic who published one novel, *Pictures From An Institution*, before his death in North Carolina as he walked along a busy highway. In one sense, many of these writers could fulfill the description given Jarrell by a fellow critic: "a self-divided southern Roman- tic."

The outstanding achievement of Tennessee literature, how- ever, was that of Knoxville-born James Agee. Impressions and experiences garnered by the bright, sensitive boy growing up in a leisurely, tree-shaded, middle-class residential area of the East Tennessee town provided him ample resource in later life for some of his best fiction. Its essence was captured in an evocative prose-poem, *Knoxville: Summer 1915,* which opened his posthumously published novel, *A Death In the Family.* In *The Morning Watch,* Agee drew on memories of his years at St. Andrews, a school for boys in Sewanee, where he formed one of the central friendships of his life, with Father James Harold Flye. Letters exchanged between the two were later published. Agee's *Let Us Now Praise Famous Men,* with photographs by Walker Evans, remains one of the original and powerful literary responses to Southern farm tenancy specifically and human need and indifference generally. It has become an American classic. Agee was also a poet, journalist, and film critic, perceptive and passionate in whatever capacity he sought to interpret life and art.

There were and are many others, among them the West Tennesseans, Peter Taylor—a master of the short story—and Jesse Hill Ford, whose novels of racial conflict won a wide national audience; and Cormac McCarthy, in the shadow of the Great Smokies, who achieved critical acclaim for his sophisticated literary skill and insight; and historian-novelist Richard Marius, whose novel, *The Coming Of Rain,* penetrated rural and small-town life in earlier decades. There was Chattanooga's writing Govan family: Gilbert Govan, a distinguished historian; Christine Noble, his wife, a popular novelist and children's writer; their daughters, Mary and Emmy, and son-in-law William O. Steele, each of whom won national awards for young people's books. Here are enough to represent that equation set out at the beginning of the chapter: ideas countering violence, spiritual exploration balancing territorial enterprise, imaginative prowess surpassing physical audacity.

As its literary interpreters were part of Tennessee education, so, too, did certain social and political events become part of that education. One looms above all others, certainly in the popular memory, because it pitted emotion against reason, faith against science, in a confrontation that expanded "education" to include the totality of life.

During the long, hot summer of 1925, the attention of Tennesseans and people around the world was focused on the little town of Dayton, thirty-five miles north of Chattanooga, where "a happening" was in progress. It was called the Monkey Trial, and it stamped an indelible image on the state.

In January 1925, William Jennings Bryan—the Great Commoner, who had received his popular nickname and adulation by championing the cause of the West, the "little man," and free silver, against the monied powers of the Northeast—made a speech in Nashville entitled "Is the Bible True?" To most Tennesseans, that was not a question, at all, but a statement of fact. Their sentiments were expressed by one of their fellow farmer-legislators, who secured a copy of Darwin's *Origin Of Species* and could not reconcile what he found there, described as evolution, with the creation described in Genesis. He introduced a bill which became law on March 21, making it illegal for any teacher in any public school in the state "to teach any theory that denies the story of the Divine Creation of man as taught in the Bible, and to teach instead that man has descended from a lower order of animals."

A few weeks later, on a warm May afternoon, a young teacher and coach at Rhea County Central High School wandered into Robinson's Drugstore, social center for the county seat of Dayton. Half a dozen men were gathered around one of the little round ice cream tables near the soda fountain. They were drinking the ubiquitous Cokes that were becoming a thirst-quenching part of the Southern way of life—and they were discussing the new law which affected the teaching of biology. Among the group was Doc Robinson, who owned the drugstore; the town's leading lawyer, Sue Hicks; and mining engineer and industrialist, Dr. George Rapplyea. They agreed that a test case of the law would be interesting and when John Scopes showed them the copy of *Civic Biology* which he had used while recently substituting for the regular biology teacher, the men asked if he would be willing to let his name be used for a test case in a court of law. Scopes agreed. Doc Robinson called the city desk of the *Chattanooga News*. "This is F. E. Robinson in Dayton," he said. "I'm chairman of the school board here. We've just arrested a man for teaching evolution." [21]

21. John T. Scopes and James Presley, *Center of the Storm: Memoirs of John T. Scopes* (New York: Holt, Rinehart & Winston, 1967), p. 60.

That was the last time anyone would have to call a newspaper's attention to Dayton. Within a few weeks, reporters from many parts of the world were filing stories from an improvised news center in the bustling town. The name of mild-mannered John Scopes became a part of history as the seething nineteenth-century war between scientific skepticism and religious dogma boiled over in this twentieth-century legal contest.

Perhaps the process was partially the result of a third force, too. In his recollection of the events leading up to his trial, Scopes later wrote that George Rappelyea was the real instigator of the lawsuit. In his orchestration of events, Rappelyea (a native New Yorker who had lived in Louisiana) convinced the businessmen of the town that the publicity of such a case would put Dayton on the map and benefit business. His was a convincing argument and the businessmen went along with it. Apparently profits as well as prophets were involved in the Monkey Trial.

On July 13, the trial began. It lasted eight days. There were two levels at which the event unfolded. One was the serious purpose that brought two famous New York lawyers—Dudley Field Malone, of Roman Catholic background, and Arthur Garfield Hays, of Jewish background—with the famous agnostic, Clarence Darrow, and a brilliant Tennessee eccentric, John Randolph Neal, along with three other attorneys, to defend Scopes. They were defending, Scopes said, the right of every person to "be free to think his own thoughts, to believe as his conscience dictated, not as someone else or the state dictated." [22]

The other level at which events proceeded was that of carnival. Dayton became a circus lot, with more than three rings in frantic action. Townspeople referred to the trial as "that monkey business" and featured countless souvenirs following that theme. The soda fountain at Robinson's Drugstore concocted a Monkey Fizz.

Every hotel and rooming house in the town was filled to capacity. Special trains carried visitors from Chattanooga. Chicago's radio station WGN set up the first nationwide radio

22. Scopes and Presley, *Center of the Storm*, p. 60.

hookup to put the listeners of America in immediate touch with Dayton, Tennessee. Twenty-two Western Union operators were at their posts in a room off a grocery store, helping provide coverage for many European countries and for China and Japan.

Among the reporters were Knoxville's own erudite humanist, Joseph Wood Krutch, who would eventually become one of the country's outstanding theater critics, essayists, and conservationists. Adolph Shelby Ochs of Chattanooga was there for his *Times*. And, most famous and abrasive, there was the Sage of Baltimore, H. L. Mencken. Mencken was already well known and well disliked in Tennessee. Following his description, five years earlier, of the South as "The Sahara of the Bozart," a Memphis editor had called Mencken a writer "as villainous of intent as he is vacant of fact." [23] The *Nashville Banner* called him merely "malicious" and "unveracious." Mencken came to Dayton with high glee and his ridicule was alternately sharp as a rapier and blunt as a cleaver. Either way, he drew blood. He was invited to leave by a group of citizens in this corner of the "Bible Belt," as he had christened the region.

Inside the courthouse and outside, too, there was material in plenty for anyone who wished to laugh or shudder, satirize or observe. There was a curious assemblage of fanatics and atheists, scholars and quacks, cranks and scientists. An advocate of the flat-earth school of geology arrived in town to promote his theory. Preachers, both home-grown and imported, beseeched, threatened and exhorted in improvised tents. Pamphleteers distributed their books—one of the most popular was *Hell And The High Schools*. Hucksters peddled their wares. Mountain men in town for "court day" aroused the curiosity and awe of outsiders who were not accustomed to seeing squirrel rifles carried on public streets.

But the chief attraction was the two antagonists: William Jennings Bryan, politician, religious fundamentalist, silver-tongued orator; and Clarence Darrow, famous defense lawyer, religious skeptic, humanitarian, wily debater. When they finally

23. Fred C. Hobson, Jr., *Serpent in Eden* (Chapel Hill: University of North Carolina Press, 1974), p. 63.

faced each other in the sweltering July heat of that tense, crowded courtroom, and on the crowded lawns outside, even the palm-leaf fans stirred more slowly and there was rapt silence among the onlookers, broken only by an unconscious gasp of shock or murmur of assent as questions and answers probed the tender nerve centers of the Bible's literal truth.

Sweat stained the shirts of the two large, intense, dedicated men locked there in verbal combat. Darrow pressed Bryan about his understanding of the serpent and creation, his notion of Joshua and the sun standing still, his belief in Jonah and a big fish, in what some reporters described as the most dramatic courtroom scene of the century. And at the end, each side apparently felt it had won. Darrow's admirers, impressed by his relentless logic and courtroom skill, and Bryan's followers, unshakeable in their faith in the True Believer, found some vindication in Dayton.

The verdict seemed an anticlimax. Each side had long since pronounced its own verdict on both the trial and its meaning. Formally, John Scopes was found guilty and fined $100. The law remained on the books until 1967, largely disregarded in textbooks and classrooms. Tennessee was fixed in the public mind as "the monkey state" for decades to come. The trial provided material for fiction, plays, and a movie.

Two items might reveal other aspects of Tennessee's encounter at Dayton. One was an observation written by H. L. Mencken after the trial. With unaccustomed charity and typical clarity, he said: "The State [Tennessee], to a degree that should be gratifying, has escaped the national standardization." Its people, he found, were quite unlike those of California or New York and, as to their religion, "they do not profess it; they believe in it." [24] Mencken granted those he had called "yokels" and "boobs" a religion that was at least not empty form and rhetoric, but something as real as their Cokes and palm-leaf fans and four-square courthouse.

The other anecdote involved a tourist who was going through Dayton, some time after the trial. He stopped to ask directions

24. Callahan, *Smoky Mountain Country,* p. 147.

of a native, then inquired flippantly, "Are there any monkeys around here?"

"No," the man replied thoughtfully, "but a lot of them pass through."

It was an answer old Hezekiah Balch or Sut Lovingood would have enjoyed.

Tennesseans have often enough resisted education on the one hand and interpretation on the other. On occasion, they have labored heroically for schools and spoken eloquently in self-discovery, self-revelation.

Samuel Doak's books on the back of his plodding horse as they crossed the mountains into the Western wilderness; Sam Houston reciting *The Iliad* and living among the Cherokees as their blood brother; Barbara Blount in her college classroom; starved little "pauper schools" struggling across the state; Night Riders at Reelfoot; Sergeant York in the Argonne Forest; Sut Lovingood's guffaws and the Fugitives' elegant protests; Bryan at Dayton and Martin Luther King at Memphis: each a small and distinct and indivisible Tennessee fragment of a whole design, an inescapable challenge.

10

The Current Frontier

*J*OHN HENDRIX and Albert Einstein had little in
common. One was an East Tennessee mountain man
who lived at the turn of the century amidst woods and
fields, country folk, legends, and a homemade world of "can-
do, make-do." The other was a Jewish scientist who moved
from Germany to America before World War II and spent much
of his life in studies and laboratories and the rarefied world of
physics, theory, and scientific speculation. But one bond joined
these two in unlikely alliance: each had a vision.

As he lay on the ground and looked up through the trees at
the sky one day in early 1900, John Hendrix heard a voice as
loud as thunder. He told his family that the voice instructed him
to sleep with his head on the ground for forty days and nights
and he would be shown visions of what the future held for the
land.

Hendrix did as he was told and shared his prophecy with his
neighbors:

> I tell you that Bear Creek Valley some day will be filled with great
> buildings and factories, and they will help toward winning the
> greatest war that will ever be. Then there will be a city on Black
> Oak Ridge, the center of everything to be a spot which is middle
> way between Sevier Tadlock's farm and Joe Pyatt's place.
>
> Railroad tracks will run between Robertsville and Scarbro.
> Thousands of people will be running to and fro. They will be build-

180

ing things and there will be a great noise and confusion and the world will shake.[1]

Some four decades later, Albert Einstein sent a memo to President Franklin D. Roosevelt. He envisioned harnessing the power of the atom. With the approval of a simple "O.K., F.D.R." and the appropriation of two billion dollars, thousands of people began running to and fro, great buildings arose at Black Oak Ridge, and, ultimately, there was a great noise, and the world shook.

A new age was born on August 6, 1945, when the United States used a hitherto unknown weapon against the city of Hiroshima, Japan, and the words *atomic bomb* and *nuclear power* became a part of popular language and public conscience. And a mysterious industrial complex tucked away in the Tennessee countryside was at the center of this historic, irreversible moment.

It was called the Manhattan Project, its end product known only to a small inner circle of scientists, government officials, and U.S. Army personnel. Although it involved thousands of workers, from mud-slogging construction crews to highly trained technicians, its purpose was one of the best-kept secrets in history.

In 1940, the population in all of Anderson County was 26,504. By June 1945, there was a raw new town in the farmlands and woods southwest of the county seat of Clinton, and its population was an estimated 75,000. Almost none knew the real purpose of his or her presence at Oak Ridge.

The secrecy worried many Tennesseans. When a Navy man home on leave from the war asked two friends working at Oak Ridge what they did there, each replied in exasperation, "I don't know!"

And when a mountain man in the vicinity told one of the scientists that rumor said the project was a new Vatican for the Pope, the scientist laughed at such a suggestion. To which the man replied, "Well, if you don't know what it is, how do you know it ain't a Vatican?"

1. Atomic Energy Historic Display at Oak Ridge Museum, Oak Ridge, Tennessee.

What it was was the nation's first uranium purifying plant, the electromagnetic separation division built under the code name *Y-12*. The people working in that plant and its related facilities represented a concentration of technical knowledge, intellectual brilliance, and monetary investment that staggered the imagination. It represented a true frontier.

Oak Ridge resembled a frontier town, too. Miles of bristling fences discouraged outsiders from exploration. Acres of mud in winter and dust in summer plagued insiders at their efforts. There were growing pains: a joke made the rounds that there were two equally prompt ways to get into Oak Ridge: stand on a corner and wait for a bus or stand in a field and wait for the town to grow up around you.

Housing for the sudden influx of people contributed to the boom-town appearance of the old West. There were barracks and dormitories, single and multi-family dwellings, trailers, "victory cottages," and a few farmhouses that had been on this land a long time. When Theodore Rockwell wrote an article in the winter of 1945 on "Frontier Life Among the Atom Splitters," he noted that "this project is run almost exclusively by youth, and its influence is felt throughout the area. The whole atmosphere of the work area is that of a university rather than a factory. Almost all the technical men up to the executive positions, are five or less years out of school; the key men are nearly all under forty-five." [2]

Among the professional people drawn from many universities and countries of the world, there was a sense of adventure, challenge, excitement. Among the blue-collar workers, drawn from a tight labor market across the South and nation, there was an air of impermanence and constant hustle. Among the people of the surrounding countryside, there was a sense of suspicion mixed with wonder. Was the real purpose of this vast undertaking some newfangled socialist experiment dreamed up by New Deal theorists? Was it a factory, as one whisper hinted, summarizing many of the shortages and prejudices of the moment,

2. Theodore Rockwell, "Frontier Life Among the Atom Splitters," *Saturday Evening Post,* December 1, 1945.

"devoted to manufacture of silk stockings, Roosevelt campaign buttons, WAAC face powder, and dehydrated water for overseas troops?" Were the private morals of those involved in this carefully guarded project in keeping with the mores of their East Tennessee neighbors?

Hostility between the newcomers and the old-timers was not as intense as might have been expected, however. One reason for the good relationship was suggested by Lt. Gen. Leslie R. Groves, head of the whole Manhattan Project, who told, more than twenty years later, why Oak Ridge was chosen as the site for the so-called Atomic City. After listing the need for a plentiful power supply, a moderate climate that would permit year-round construction, and an inland location lessening vulnerability from sea or air attack by enemies, plus reasonable land prices, he concluded:

> Above all, I knew that the labor supply of East Tennessee was of a very high order from the standpoint of willingness to work. And, I knew that if we had to use many female operators—and I didn't anticipate as many as we actually required—Tennessee girls would be much more easily trained and would do better work than those of some other sections of the country. The principal reason for this was that the women here were not so sophisticated—they hadn't been reared to believe they "knew it all." [3]

General Groves's statement possibly revealed more than he intended, both about the status of Tennessee's working women and himself, but it was true that each welcomed the other in those early years of the 1940s.

A physicist named J. H. Rush later affirmed the respect many of the scientists and newcomers to the region came to hold for the local participants in their mutual undertaking. Rush decided that the people in the project

> who impressed me most were not the scientists, who knew approximately what they were doing, but the laborers, who didn't. Our experiments often required setting up cumbersome apparatus in situations that involved exposure to atomic radiation. The maintenance

3. Knoxville *Journal,* September 5, 1967.

men who helped us on such jobs might be required to wear dust masks or to come out of a hazardous area after thirty minutes or an hour, while technicians nosed about with radiation counters. To these laborers—many of them poorly educated men from the local farm country—the intimations of mysterious, invisible danger must have been impressive. Yet I never saw one of them refuse a task, or show any uneasiness in exposing himself to the unknown hazard.[4]

Thus physicists on a new frontier and farm folk from an old frontier joined in an effort that resulted in the birth of another age for all humankind.

Dimensions of that age have dawned only slowly on public consciousness and private consciences. Physicist Rush considered these and concluded that use of the atomic bomb had obscured "the real meaning of the Manhattan District Project. What it signified was that mankind was moving into a new order of power over itself and the environment, and that henceforth the consequences of man's acts must be weighed with utmost caution."[5]

There was a profound order of appropriateness in the development of the new Atomic City in the ancient Southern Appalachian area. Here past and future merged in an intense culmination of all those weapons and battles the Volunteers had relied on so fervently over generations, merged in an incredible prophecy of doom—or fulfillment. Subsequent developments and continuing research at Oak Ridge would expand the horizons of each possibility, placing more firmly in the human grasp the tools with which to play God.

The vision John Hendrix had received through a voice as of thunder and the vision achieved through Albert Einstein's imagination and intellect had met on the Black Oak Ridge in Tennessee. Each symbolized the changes that were accelerating and intensifying all across the state. Tennessee's cartoon stereotype as a calcified stronghold of all that was past and backward had never been accurate, of course. The state's experience with change was considerable. As part of the West, it had known the

4. J. H. Rush, "Prometheus in Tennessee," *Saturday Review*, July 2, 1960, p. 11.
5. Rush, "Prometheus in Tennessee," p. 50.

changes accompanying many phases of settlement and recurring developments of land and commerce; as part of the South, it had suffered the changes and a bitter aftermath wrought by war on its own soil; as a rural state, it had been subject to the devastating changes visited by nature's forces (boll weevil to cotton, drought to corn, black shank to tobacco) and man's machinations (panics and depressions hurting the dirt-farmers first and longest); as an urban state, it had accumulated the changes multiplied by four metropolitan areas expanding and vying for industry, for all the prizes and penalties of growth.

One of the most innovative catalysts for change in Tennessee was, of course, the Tennessee Valley Authority. The valley of the mighty Tennessee River was, in 1930, the most poverty-stricken major river basin in the United States. Annual personal income averaged $317, 45 percent of the national average. Much of the valuable land was eroded or in a poor state of cultivation; floods ravaged many of the farms, towns, and cities along the Tennessee's course and farther downstream, after it added its swollen waters to the Ohio and Mississippi at their floodtide; navigation on the river and its tributaries was erratic and diminishing; use of electric power was limited, nonexistent in many rural areas.

Seeking to meet these needs and make use of an abandoned hydroelectric project that had been built at the wild Muscle Shoals rapids in northwest Alabama during World War I, President Franklin D. Roosevelt, prompted by Nebraska Senator George W. Norris, sent a historic message to Congress on April 10, 1933. His appeal was couched in terms characteristically shrewd and idealistic:

> The continued idleness of a great national investment in the Tennessee Valley leads me to ask the Congress for legislation necessary to enlist this project in the service of the people.
> It is clear that the Muscle Shoals development is but a small part of the potential public usefulness of the entire Tennessee River.
> Such use, if envisioned in its entirety, transcends mere power development: it enters the wide fields of flood control, soil erosion, afforestation, elimination from agricultural use of marginal lands, and distribution and diversification of industry. In short, this power de-

velopment of war days leads logically to national planning for a complete river watershed involving many States and the future lives and welfare of millions. It touches and gives life to all forms of human concerns.

I, therefore, suggest to the Congress, legislation to create a Tennessee Valley Authority—a corporation clothed with the power of government but possessed of the flexibility and initiative of a private enterprise. It should be charged with the broadest duty of planning for the proper use, conservation, and development of the natural resources of the Tennessee River drainage basin and its adjoining territory for the general social and economic welfare of the Nation.[6]

Thus, in the 1930s, Tennessee frontiersmen exchanged the coonskin caps of the long hunters for the hard hats of the TVA. There was considerable irony in the fact that one of the most comprehensive resource-planning programs in history should be centered in a region whose people were traditionally hostile to any "planning." Jealous of the slightest encroachment on their private liberties, Tennesseans traditionally resented interference by revenuers, would-be uplifters, and experts of any stripe. But as the valley's people and TVA came to know each other, they discovered that they were working with each other for a common goal.

A giant stairway of dams and reservoirs took shape in the 40,000 square miles of the Tennessee River watershed. "The Great Lakes of the South" were created. Floods abated. By 1974, TVA could estimate $1.3 billion in benefits attributable to its flood control system over the years.

Power began to flow up the hills and hollows, into the small towns and the huge industries that came because of that supply—the vast complex at Oak Ridge, as an example. By 1974, TVA's sales of electricity amounted to 106 billion kilowatt-hours a year.

Navigation increased and brought renewed activity along a number of waterfronts, reaching a total of 29 million tons of freight in 1974. Land and forest use improved dramatically and

6. Arthur E. Morgan, *The Making of the T.V.A.* (Buffalo: Prometheus Books, 1974), p. 2.

included a vast fertilizer development, woods-products expansion, and recreational research and management.

Specific experience and practical information combined with an innovative continuing sense of mission—and TVA became known, at home and around the world, as a "yardstick," not only for cheaper power, but for effective planning on a broad regional level. Perhaps the most important power harnessed by TVA was that described by a Southern newspaperman who said that "the significant advance has been made in the thinking of the people. They are no longer afraid. They have caught the vision of their own power." [7]

TVA has not been perfect, however, nor free of controversy. From the moment of its inception until today, it has spawned debate, ranging from personal dissatisfactions to large national issues. Landowners who did not want to leave their homes and familiar acres resisted "heartless" surveyors and land-buyers. Private power interests fought arrival of a government-owned competitor. Within the first board of directors, there were basic philosophic conflicts between chairman Arthur E. Morgan and co-director David E. Lilienthal. Later, there was a titanic political struggle between "outsider" Lilienthal and Tennessee's powerful native son, U.S. Senator Kenneth D. McKellar. Their battle has been described as the difference between two democracies, that of the cracker-barrel and that of the pork-barrel.

In recent years, many of the conservation forces that were once the nucleus of TVA's stoutest support have become increasingly alienated by TVA's large consumption of strip-mined coal in its steam plants and its marginal attention to environmental concerns. As power production has grown from its originally subordinate purpose to the chief commitment of TVA, the dilemma has posed hard choices. That cheap power that TVA is expected to produce requires cheap coal. Much of this is strip-mined coal. Strip-mining destroys much of the very earth, water, and natural habitat that TVA was originally dedicated to restore and preserve. Conservationists assert that TVA reclamation standards have been either inadequate or neglected. TVA

7. Callahan, *Smoky Mountain Country*, p. 183.

responds that the realities of its budget allow only a certain amount of reclamation investment. It is useful for both critics and defenders to realize that the existence and the priorities of TVA are determined, in the long run, by the people of the United States and their government. Neither sacrosanct nor iniquitous, it may be a mirror, returning to Tennessee and the nation a self-image.

In the beginning, a spirit of high purpose and initiative surrounded TVA. Today, it often appears as an embattled giant—so quickly, from the 1930s to the 1970s, does the supposed radical become the reputed reactionary. One generation's energized enlightenment becomes another generation's entrenched establishment. What is especially interesting here is that the choices faced by TVA now—including the major national and international issue of nuclear power and breeder reactor plants, with attendant riches of energy and threats of holocaust—should be focused, to an important extent, in Tennessee. Once again, the state represents a frontier.

Orderly figures of census reports confirm another recent revolution that has shaken the state. In 1950, Tennessee was 55.9 percent rural. In 1960, it was 52.3 percent urban. During that decade, Tennesseans had joined a growing trend and, literally, gone to town. Following the example of many adjoining states, in one of the greatest migrations in the nation's history, they had also discovered many of the accompanying consequences. These touched every facet of Tennessee life.

As farms changed, machinery replaced men and animals. The mule—once balky symbol of all that was essential to cultivation of the land—virtually disappeared. And with the mule went swapping-days and blacksmith shops and the legendary Columbia Mule Day, and a slower pace within the turning of the seasons. As people clustered closer in cities or suburbs, they often grew more distant in personal relationships. The family storyteller, local history buff, neighbor musician was replaced by the canned, everyday entertainment of radio and television. Children were born in clinics, and old people died in institutions, and there were official channels to meet human needs and hungers that seemed to grow ever more remote, more removed from public awareness. Progress brought by mechanization was imposing its penalties of congestion and pollution as well as its benefits of relief from drudgery. The need for pause, for evaluation and choice, was perhaps part of the cry voiced by a country woman who said that she didn't want to be bothered by any more of "these modern inconveniences."

The pace of change continued. By 1970 Tennessee was 58.7 percent urban. Neither the reality nor the rate of such a major shift in population had been anticipated, even by the forecasters and social seers of TVA. An architect-designer reported in 1970 that director David Lilienthal once told him that "the TVA had not anticipated the great migration to the city; and that TVA had a multiple-use resource policy for rural development but no urban policy." [8]

Neither was there any policy for an institution or agency regarding major racial shifts in population. This was another radical change uprooting Tennessee life.

The story was told in West Tennessee of a plantation owner who lost his last tenant from the cotton fields. As the jubilant black man departed for Chicago, "to shake the money-tree," he emphasized to his former employer his new liberation: "I'm not reckoning on ever again saying 'Get up' to a mule—unless it's settin' in my lap."

Many Negroes left farms and piney woods and broomsedge fields of Tennessee to hit the big cities North and West and East. Others crowded into the state's cities: 64.1 percent of Tennessee's black population was in cities in 1950; 80.1 percent, in 1970. Their distribution reflected the three distinctive regions of the state: 37 percent of Memphis's population was black in 1970; 17 percent of Nashville's, 16 percent of Chattanooga's, and 7 percent of Knoxville's.

Suddenly, Tennessee began to realize that it was no longer a rural state of country folks living country ways. Just as the great livestock drives through the mountains from the nation's hog-and-hominy range of Tennessee to lowland markets in South

---

8. Gerald M. McCue, William R. Ewald, Jr., and the Midwest Research Institute, *Creating the Human Environment* (Urbana: University of Illinois Press, 1970), p. 11.

Carolina and Georgia had been replaced long since by gleaming rails of steel and swaying boxcars, so, too, the colorful commerce and romance, mischief and mystery of the Natchez Trace, the so-called Devil's Backbone running from Nashville to Natchez, Mississippi, had been long ago supplanted by asphalt and concrete thoroughfares. Whistles on the rivers' proud steamboats, beckoning landlocked farmers and villagers from surrounding countryside, had yielded to the blast of horns on lumbering trucks and surging cars. Church sociables and school entertainments did not draw the crowds that were turning to country clubs and drive-ins sprung up like mushrooms in recent pastures, cornfields, woodlots. Small enterprises begun in Tennessee had become household names around the country and the world: Maxwell House, Jack Daniels, Genesco, Stokely-Van Camp, Holiday Inns. Big industry sent branches into Tennessee and manufactured steel and cars, aluminum and textiles, chemicals, paper and electrical equipment, among others on a lengthening roll-call of products.

In addition to Tennessee's four major cities, there were rapidly growing metropolitan areas embracing smaller cities—two, in particular: Kingsport-Bristol, bordering on Virginia, and Clarksville-Hopkinsville, reaching into Kentucky.

The little fort near the French Lick, where James Robertson had planted a crop of corn in 1779, was now—after considerable early shifting between Knoxville, Kingston, Murfreesboro—the capital of the state. Nashville was: spacious, greening horse pastures and cattle farms of the surrounding countryside; college and university campuses; gleaming banks and insurance buildings; a replica of the Parthenon; Cheekwood Art Museum and Botanical Gardens; ancient red-brick Ryman Auditorium and plush new museum of country music; and on the city's highest hill, the Capitol, modeled after an Ionic temple, with a burgeoning plaza and state office building offering the nation's first state Center for the Performing Arts.

White's Fort was no longer the East Tennessee settlement surveyed in 1783, the frontier of a land boom as veterans of the Revolutionary War sought their claims for vast virgin acres, no longer a way-station on the south fork of the Wilderness Road, patronized by pioneers journeying west, terrorized by the murderous Big Harpe and Little Harpe, outlaws of eighteenth-century Manson viciousness. Knoxville was the industrial contrast of marble mills and textiles, the University of Tennessee and TVA headquarters, Neyland Stadium at the heart of "Big Orange" country, and tobacco warehouses loud with autumn market chants among pungent stacks of golden-brown leaves.

Ross's Landing, picturesque beside the great Moccasin Bend of the Tennessee River, beneath the towering escarpment of Lookout Mountain and the walls of Missionary Ridge and Signal Mountain, was no longer a Cherokee trading center or a military post of embarkation for the cruel Trail of Tears westward. It was no small town, booming as Northern soldiers returned to the village and countryside they had fought over during the Civil War, as Northern capitalists discovered the potential of resources and geography here. Chattanooga was a center of railroads and foundries, patent medicine and soft drinks, homes and prep schools and historical battlegrounds perched on mountain tops and slopes, edging into Georgia, peaking out in the clouds.

The western city on the Fourth Chickasaw Bluff was no longer a brawling river-town where yellow fever epidemics decimated the population and enmity smouldered between the "Pinch" of north Memphis (where the underfed residents on Catfish Bay reportedly "pinched their guts" with their belts to relieve their hunger) and the "Sodom" of a reputedly wicked south Memphis. Memphis was the proudly clean and noise-free metropolitan center for adjoining northwest Mississippi and eastern Arkansas, as well as being Tennessee's largest city. Memphis was hardwood center of the nation, and host to Cotton Carnival, memorial to the days of single-crop rule when the trade and exchange buildings on Front Street had been the commercial heart of the cotton kingdom. By 1968, tobacco and soybeans had replaced cotton as king on Tennessee's farms. Memphis was big industry.

Memphis was a skyscraper with a slowly revolving cocktail lounge that allowed its patrons to look over green Overton Park and the stadium shaped like a sombrero, and all the plants, offices, buildings of trade and learning, and the mighty steel sweep of bridge spanning the wide, moving expanse of Ol'Man River. And in the gradual turning, the viewer could look north, where the French first floated down through the heart of America; and east, where the trails once reached back to the huddled little English settlements; and south, where the Spanish had probed up the river hoping for empire; and finally west—the west that stretches out to the horizon and was once frontier.

Now the viewer knows that the frontier is not "out *there*," has not been for a long time, but is *here*. It is a frontier of mind and purpose and will.

Some would reject any frontier, abandoning strengths and problems compounded from the buried past, abdicating responsibility for the beckoning future. To them, the question would have to be posed: was the historian of early Tennessee correct when he said, "The frontier is most aptly characterized not by the cry of the frontiersman for more freedom, but by the cry of the speculator for more land." [9] If that insatiable, unabated appetite for land continues, today and tomorrow, how shall we respond to the speculating, the destroying or the conserving, the cherishing of real, tangible, irreplaceable earth and water and air and their resources by which we survive or perish?

Some would return to old frontiers, seeking, through a new primitivism, escape from inescapable choices.

Some would meet the new frontiers with old perspectives, not yet grasping the full significance of scientist Rush's realization at Oak Ridge that humanity has moved into a new order of power over itself and the environment.

Confidence in the ability of Tennesseans to meet challenges was voiced long ago by a shrewd visitor to the state. Aaron Burr said, "Tennesseans, as the breed runs in 1806, can go anywhere and do anything." [10]

Sooner than they could have expected, the question changed: not what could they do, but what would they do.

Historians have pointed out that nothing was more in demand

9. Abernethy, *Frontier to Plantation*, p. 359.
10. J. T. Moore, *Tennessee, the Volunteer State*, p. 37.

on the frontier of the Old Southwest than strong leadership. Strength alone is no longer sufficient. The intensifying complexity of life, the terrible capability for death which humans now hold, demands that today's frontiersmen be wise, as well as strong. The questions they face are awesome. How shall we use and not misuse the human and natural resources that are our heritage and our bequest to the future? How shall we govern ourselves most responsively and responsibly at the local level so that we shall not create vacuums inviting outside control? How shall we remain unique in our proud individuality, and humble in our common humanity?

These and similar considerations crowd the imagination. They are not trivial or peripheral. They will determine what kind of state Tennesseans want, what kind of Tennessee they will have. And that, multiplied by fifty other answers, will determine what kind of America we have during the third century of our national life.

Finally, it might be tonic to remember an old saying common among East Tennesseans: "That lawsuit may be settled at the courthouse, but it's not been settled up the holler yet."

That's where our answers will be determined eventually: up the hollow, alley, street and lane, thoroughfare, and skyway, in each individual memory and character and commitment.

That seems an even more exciting vision than the one imagined by Christian Priber, who brought his plan of a place called Paradise to the Cherokees in Tennessee before any white man had settled there, more stirring than the vision dreamed a century and a half later by John Hendrix, who foresaw a town on the Black Oak Ridge—to be called Paradise. Tennessee has not been, nor will it be paradise. It has not birthed saints or devils. But in its three grand divisions and bountiful variety, it can be what it has been: a very human place. With decision "up the hollow," it can become an even better place.

Suggestions For Further Reading

Anyone seeking an acquaintance with Tennessee's past would be wise to read *A Guide to the Study and Reading of Tennessee History* by William T. Alderson and Robert H. White (Nashville: Tennessee Historical Commission, 1959), a succinct, selective 87 pages; and *Tennessee History, A Bibliography*, by Sam B. Smith (Knoxville: University of Tennessee Press, 1974), clear and comprehensive in 498 pages.

Of several multivolume histories of the state, one of the best is *Tennessee: A History, 1673–1932*, by Philip M. Hamer (New York: American Historical Society, 1933). *Tennessee, A Short History*, by Stanley J. Folmsbee, Robert E. Corlew, and Enoch L. Mitchell (Knoxville: University of Tennessee Press, 1969, 1972) is the standard one-volume authority. In 1886 and 1887, the Goodspeed Publishing Company of Nashville issued, in six volumes, *A History of Tennessee from the Earliest Times to the President*. A narrative of the state from frontier days to the Civil War and of selected groups of counties appears in each volume. Although there were deviations from total accuracy, the detailed accounts were of sufficient interest to be reprinted in the early 1970s by Charles and Randy Elder of Nashville.

Among works examining Tennessee's prehistory and Indian past, three indispensable volumes are *Tribes That Slumber: Indians of the Tennessee Region*, by Thomas M. N. Lewis and Madeline Kneberg (Knoxville: University of Tennessee Press, 1958); *The Cherokee Nation of Indians*, by Charles C. Royce, included in the Fifth Annual Report of the Bureau of Ethnology, 1883–1884 (Washington, D.C.: Government Printing Office, 1887); and James Mooney's *Myths of the Cherokee*, American Indian History Series (1900; reprint edition, St. Clair, Mich., Scholarly Press, 1970), part of the nineteenth Annual Report of the Bureau of American Ethnology. Also interesting are John R. Swanton's *The Indians of the Southeastern United States*, Smithsonian Institution, Bureau of American Ethnology Bulletin 137

(Washington, D.C.: Government Printing Office, 1946); and John P. Brown's *Old Frontiers* (Kingsport: Southern, 1938).

Three important early historians are John Haywood, who wrote *The Natural and Aboriginal History of Tennessee up to the First Settlements Therein by the White People, in the Year 1768* (Nashville: G. Wilson, 1823) and *Civil and Political History of the State of Tennessee from Its Earliest Settlement up to the Year 1796 Including the Boundaries of the State*, First American Frontier Series (1823; reprint edition, New York: Arno Press, 1971); James G. M. Ramsey, *Annals of Tennessee to the End of the Eighteenth Century*, First American Frontier Series (1853; reprint edition, New York: Arno Press, 1971); and A. W. Putnam, *History of Middle Tennessee: Or, Life & Times of General James Robertson*, Tennesseana Editions Series (1859; reprint edition, Knoxville: University of Tennessee Press, 1971).

Samuel Cole Williams, called "the most productive writer of Tennessee history," elicits from fellow historians both critical dismissal and professional acceptance. Among his books that taught me much about the state are *Beginnings of West Tennessee, in the Land of the Chickasaws, 1541–1814* (Johnson City: Watauga, 1930); *Dawn of Tennessee Valley and Tennessee History, 1541–1776* (Johnson City: Watauga, 1937); and *History of the Lost State of Franklin*, revised edition, Perspectives in American History Series, No. 23 (1924, 1933; reprint edition, Philadelphia: Porcupine Press, 1973).

Beyond debate is the value of several books on specific topics: *King's Mountain and Its Heroes: History of the Battle of King's Mountain October 7th, 1780, & the Events Which Led to It*, by Lyman C. Draper (1881; reprint edition, Baltimore: Genealogical Publishing Co., 1971); *William Blount*, by William Masterson (1954; reprint edition, Westport, Conn.: Greenwood Press, 1970); *From Frontier to Plantation*, by Thomas P. Abernethy (Chapel Hill: University of North Carolina Press, 1932); *John Sevier: Pioneer of the Old Southwest*, by Carl S. Driver (Chapel Hill: University of North Carolina Press, 1932); *Life of Andrew Jackson*, by James Parton (1860; reprint edition, New York: Johnson Reprint Corp., 1972); and *The Life of Andrew Jackson*, by John Spencer Bassett (Garden City, N.Y.: 1911); *The Raven: A Biography of Sam Houston*, by Marquis James (Dunwoody, Ga.: Norman S. Berg, Publisher, 1968); *The Army of Tennessee: A Military History*, by Stanley F. Horn (1953; reprint edition,

Norman, Okla.: University of Oklahoma Press, 1968); *Unionism and Reconstruction in Tennessee, 1860–1869*, by James W. Patton (Gloucester, Mass.: Peter Smith, Publisher, 1934); *The Woman's Suffrage Movement in Tennessee*, by Antoinette Elizabeth Taylor (New York: Bookman, 1957); and *Tennessee: A Guide to the State*, compiled by the Federal Writers' Project of the WPA (New York: Viking Press, 1939)—a book both general and specific.

Concerning the state's division into three distinctive regions, these books are interesting: *The Biography of a River Town: Memphis: Its Heroic Age*, by Gerald M. Capers, Jr. (Chapel Hill: University of North Carolina Press, 1939); *Old Times in West Tennessee*, by Joseph S. Williams (Memphis: W. G. Gheeney, 1873); Harriette Simpson Arnow's *Seedtime on the Cumberland* and *Flowering of the Cumberland* (New York: Macmillan, 1960 and 1963); *The Tennessee, The Old River: Frontier to Secession*, Rivers of America Series (New York: Holt, Rinehart and Winston, 1946); *The Chattanooga Country, 1540–1951*, by Gilbert E. Govan and James W. Livingood (New York: Dutton, 1952); *The French Broad-Holston Country*, by Mary U. Rothrock (Knoxville: East Tennessee Historical Society, 1946); *Knoxville*, by Betsy Beeler Creekmore (Knoxville: University of Tennessee Press, 1967); and Paul J. Vanderwood's *The Night Riders of Reelfoot Lake* (Memphis: Memphis State University Press, 1969).

Index

199

DATE DUE
